Sacred Tears

Fanitra Brantley

authorHOUSE®

AuthorHouse™
1663 Liberty Drive
Bloomington, IN 47403
www.authorhouse.com
Phone: 1 (800) 839-8640

Published by AuthorHouse 02/02/2016

ISBN: 978-1-5049-7594-0 (sc)
ISBN: 978-1-5049-7595-7 (e)

Dedication

I dedicate this book to the man who introduced my heart to the love of Jesus Christ, my beloved grandfather, Rev. Dr. E. L. Hart, Sr. There is not a day that goes by that I do not think about you. You were indeed a man after God's own heart! I am so proud to have your blood running through my veins. Thanks for being and setting the example of a true Godly man. I can only hope to be half the person you were! Until we meet again, Pop-Pop, please "Save a seat for me!" I love you!

Acknowledgements

Many people have blessed and helped me along my journey. Most importantly, I want to thank my best friend; One who was there for me even when I did not realize it. Thank you, Jesus, for all you have done and continue to do for me. I could never repay You for Your unconditional love. I will forever give You all the honor and praise, because if it had not been for You on my side...where would I be? Without You, Jesus, I am nothing!

I would like to thank Pastor Darnell A. Brantley, Sr. This book would not have been possible without you! I know it was not easy, but I thank you for your love, support and encouragement throughout this process; it meant the world to me! We have laughed. We have cried. We have asked for forgiveness. In the end, we know the love and respect we share for each other, and for God, will always prevail. You were the first person to call me "your" 1st Lady. I cherish the memories we have shared together. We have experienced some "mountaintop" and some "rough side of the mountain" times. But I count them all joy, because the good will always outweigh the bad in my heart. Our life lessons have helped me become the beautiful, God-fearing woman I am today! I have grown as a Christian because of your God-given teachings and sermons, and I am now able to teach others about the goodness of the Lord! Together, God has used us to do many mighty works for His Kingdom and win countless souls for Christ. I will forever love the God that dwells in you! I will spend a lifetime thanking you for blessing me with our four beautiful children!

I would like to thank my four precious heartbeats - my children! Zayla, Darnell Jr., Faith & Destiny - You are my reason for breathing; my reason to live! You are my joy! Being your mother will always be my greatest accomplishment on earth. I love you with all of my heart and soul! Always remember if you put God first in your lives, you will be able to overcome anything! Never underestimate the love God has for you!

I would like to thank my mother, Myra, and father, Leon. I could not have asked for better parents. I am grateful for the sacrifices you made for me. Thanks for loving me and showing me how to love others. The love I have for my family, and passion for helping others, came from the two of you. It is an honor and privilege to be your daughter!

I would like to thank my brothers and sister, Quentin, Jacque and Lenore. I am so proud to be the older sister of three amazing souls! You all inspire me to want to make you proud of me. I love you!

I would like to give a very special thank you to the two Proverbs 31 women in my life, my beautiful grandmothers, Ruby Roman and 1st Lady Pearl Hart. You are my jewels! I thank you for all the wisdom and knowledge you have shared with me over the years. Your words have been food to my soul, and I will always cherish them.

I would like to thank my cousin, Lakeisha Loving, for being the big sister I have never had! You helped to make my childhood memories awesome! You have always supported me in everything I have done! Your love is immeasurable!

I would like to thank my mentor, sister/friend-for-life, Author Mirthell Bazemore! You were sent by God! I appreciate your constant encouragement throughout the process of writing this book. I am grateful you saw the writer God placed inside of me. I cannot thank you enough for your guidance, and love you have displayed to me and my family!

I would like to thank my best friend, Rasheeda Usry! Thank you for being my "close friend," a listening ear and a shoulder to cry on. I praise God for our David/Johnathan relationship! You will never know how much your friendship means to me! I love you, Sis!

I would like to thank my co-host and friend for life, John L. Sanders! You are a blessing to my life in so many ways! Thanks for believing in me!

I would like to thank Pastor Vizion Jones for your prayers, support and allowing God to use you to introduce me to some amazing people!

I would like to thank Bishop T. D. Jakes for your on-time, God-given sermons that helped to nourish my soul back to health. I will forever be grateful for your ministry!

I would like to thank M.O. G. Murvin and J. Murvin Records. Your love and support is a blessing tome and my ministry!

I would like to thank photographer, Kaz Artiz of Zionimages, for always taking my visions and making them come to life! I also would like to thank photographer Al G. Sillah, for capturing me deep in thought.

Last, but not least, I would like to thank Kim Mathis & family, as well as the Romans, Harts, Derricotts, Rawls, Brantleys, McGhaws and all Church members and friends who have supported me and my family throughout the years…I love you! May God abundantly bless each of you beyond measure!

Contents

Drama Queen!

I never would have thought in a million years I would be writing a book about my life. I was born and raised in Atlanta, for most of my life. As a child, I was shy - EXTREMELY SHY! I never liked taking pictures. When it was time to take pictures, I would either run or hide behind someone! In fact, there are many pictures of me running from taking a picture. I never wanted to be in the spotlight; I was perfectly fine being in the background or not participating at all. I enjoyed being a cheerleading for the people who actually wanted to participate in activities, because I was never a jealous person. I loved watching the people around me doing what they desired to do. I was content seeing others doing well.

As far as I can remember, I have always been different. For example, I always wanted my mother to make my clothes. If everyone was wearing the same style shoe, I wanted to wear something else. I was never the child who did something because everyone else was doing it; there had to be a reason for me to do it. It had to make sense in my mind. I always did the opposite of everyone else...on purpose! A prime example is I would not recite Easter speeches in Church, no matter how many times my family chastised me. I would stand in front of the Church and not utter a mumbling word! As soon as Church was over, I would say my Easter speech - loudly and clearly - on the way home. My parents would be so aggravated! They would fuss at me and tell me to hush, because if I could say it in the car, I could have said it in the Church!

I came from a churchgoing family. My father's mother was a deaconess/mother and my mother's father was a pastor. No matter how hard they tried to convince me, I would never sing in the choir or usher. No…sorry. I was not going to do it! My family finally stopped asking me to do things in Church, because they knew I was not going to do them and I would embarrass the heck out of them! I was even the last one to get baptized out of my siblings and first cousins…on purpose! While everyone was running to get baptized, I was running away from baptism because no one could tell me why I "had" to get baptized. What was the purpose of being baptized? I was not doing anything that anyone told me I "had" to do, if they could not explain the reason why I had to do it. I was often told I was "destined for hell," because I was not baptized. Frankly, at the time, I did not care.

It was not until I heard my grandfather preach an entire sermon on baptism, that I wanted to be baptized on my own - without being forced. His sermon answered all my questions. His sermon introduced me to Jesus. The day I was baptized, the Mother's Board and Deaconesses shouted for joy. I cannot begin to tell you how many times I had run away from them, out of the Baptism Preparatory room. To them, I had the devil in me! At a certain point they stopped chasing me, saying, "Let her go, she'll be back once the Spirit hits her!" Their words turned out to be extremely accurate!

As you can see, I was never into doing things outside of my comfort zone. The first time I surprised myself by doing something outside of the normal was when I joined the Drama Club at school. I was introduced to the Drama Club by tagging along with my best friend. After sitting in on a few classes, acting looked fun so I decided to join. Shortly thereafter, I discovered I had a natural gift for acting. No one, especially my family, could believe I was on a stage speaking and performing in front of hundreds of people. I even had a hard time believing it! On stage, I felt empowered. I was not myself on stage; something else came over me. Acting gave me an adrenaline rush. I was able to recite my lines with a boldness I had never experienced prior to that moment. For a brief moment in time, I was someone else. Who was that girl? Where did she come from? What happened to my shyness?

Acting was scary, yet it was fun. Within the Drama Club, I made friends with people who were just as "different" as me. Before joining the Drama Club, I felt as if no one understood me. Now, I had finally found a place where I belonged; where I did not have to be someone else's cheerleader. I no longer had to tag along with someone else on their "thing." Drama Club was my thing and I loved it!

Just when I thought life was looking up, it all fell apart. My parents decided to split...again; which meant we had to move... again. Prior to this split, my parents had separated numerous times, which had caused me to go to several different schools. I thought I was finally done with being the "new girl" in school. Unfortunately, I was mistaken. I was extremely disappointed because I had finally found an activity that I excelled at and enjoyed! As quickly as I found the Drama Club, it was taken away from me. There was nothing I could do about the matter. It is not like I had a say so – I was a child. Although I completely understand my parent's decisions, now that I am an adult, I was too young to understand why we had to move at the time. When I joined my new school's Drama Department IT WAS NOT THE SAME! I hated it with a passion! I disliked it so much that I used to skip the classes. I no longer wanted to participate in any of the Drama activities. The passion and fire I once had for Drama activities had extinguished. I will never know how far I could have made it as an actress.

As I reflect upon this period in my life, it almost runs parallel with my life today and the things I have experienced the past few years. It seems that in my adult life, just like when I was a child, as soon as I felt a sense of belonging and passion, it was abruptly stripped away from me. Here are some of the questions I have had to ask my adult self: Do I become defeated again or do I use all that

I have been through to help others who may be going through the things I have experienced? Do I let the devil silence my voice again or do I let God use my voice as a spiritual mouthpiece for those who are too shy, too afraid or too ashamed to tell their stories? Do I go back to hiding behind others or do I step into the spotlight and trust God to be the Director of my life? If you are reading this book, you can see how I have answered my questions. Here is my testimony of how I used my pain to discover my God-given purpose.

Preacher's Wife? Who...Me?

Some women, in parts of the South and Bible Belt, think it is an honor and privilege to be married to a Minister. In fact, in some Churches, the Senior Pastor's wife is called the "1st Lady." The term is used out of respect for being the wife of the head leader of the Church. Becoming a 1st Lady, in some eyes of churchgoers, is like becoming a queen of a small country of some sort. A lot of women are raised to be 1st Ladies. That's right...raised! By that, I mean they are told by their parents or guardians that they are going to become a "Preacher's Wife." In those parents or guardian's eyes, no other man on earth is good enough for their daughters. Those types of people can become so obsessed with wanting their daughters to marry a preacher that they will go to great lengths or depths to make it possible. They mistakenly believe the marriage will give them some type of prominence above "regular" churchgoers. Their faulty logic makes them think a title gives them a better chance of entering Heaven. In my opinion, that concept is nothing new. Two of the disciples (James and John), went back and forth over a similar issue when they argued about sitting on the right side and left side of Jesus. Thankfully, Jesus nipped their nonsense in the bud and set the example. If you are a Christian, you should know that God is not concerned with titles or positions. Unfortunately, there are delusional people who think being close to Ministers/Pastors makes them better than others.

I know of families who moved their membership to Churches that had single Ministers/Pastors to better the chances of their daughter(s) getting chosen to become a Minister's Wife. On the flip side, I know of women who abruptly left Churches because the single Minister/Pastor chose someone else as a spouse. Unfortunately, I also know of women who prey on married Ministers/Pastors, with the hopes of getting them to leave their wives and marry them. That is a dangerous mindset. No one should be more in love with the man/woman of God than they are with the God that dwells in the man/woman of God. One has to be careful when it comes to the transferring of feelings and emotions for God to Ministers/Pastors. If a person is not careful, they will end up idolizing the man/woman of God. At that point, they are no longer worshiping God; they are worshipping a man/woman. On the flip side, ALL Ministers/Pastors should have the knowledge, training and "know how" to deal with the transference of emotions and not take advantage of people who knowingly or unknowingly idolize them. Ministers/Pastors are called to lead people to God, not turn themselves into a god for people to worship.

Personally, I never had a desire to become a Minister's Wife. As a grandchild of a Pastor, I was able to witness the glamourous and not so glamourous sides of being a 1st Lady, first hand. I watched how sometimes the 1st Lady role could be exciting, and at other times it could be very difficult and downright depressing! I saw that being a 1st Lady could also be very lonely. I noticed friends come and go out of my grandmother's life. I viewed Church members praise her for being a dedicated hard worker, then I observed some of the same Church members talk about her, saying she was trying to take over. I witnessed how she had to share her husband with the Church. Vacations and family events were often cut short, because the work of the Lord came first. My grandmother's entire life revolved around the Church. It was like watching her ride a roller-coaster of emotional highs and lows. Based on my perspective, I came to the conclusion that being a 1st Lady was a calling from God. Most women could not handle the responsibilities that came along with the title. Therefore, it was to my surprise that I - the sprint runner from the Lord, the black sheep that hated to participate in Church activities - ended up becoming a Minister's Wife and a 1ˢᵗ Lady. It was just as puzzling and confusing to me as it may be to you right now!

My husband and I met in the Church that my beloved grandfather pastored. My husband was a Minister and he also served in the US Navy's elite Submarine Force. The fact that he was a Minister did not bother me. I did not see it as being anything special because being a part of a "First Family" meant I was often around a lot of Ministers. Any given day, there would be Ministers "fellowshipping" at my grandparents' house with our family. My grandparents treated them all as family and taught us to do the same. When you are around Minsters all the time, you get to see what most churchgoers do not see...the human side of them! When I met my husband, he was 20 years old and I was 18 years old. He was handsome, charming and extraordinarily charismatic. He was a genuine gentleman, especially to be so young. He was an overall great guy and a true people person. My husband had a way of touching the hearts of everyone he met. He was one of those people that you wanted in your life as a friend. Everywhere he went, he made a positive, lasting impression on others. He knew how to make me laugh, which was a plus, yet he could be very serious when it came to certain issues. We would talk about anything and everything. No subject was off limits. Being "the new girl," I was used to being judged by others. But he never judged me; nor did I judge him.

On our very first date he called and asked if I would like to accompany him to the mall. Mall? Sure! I was 18 years old and still in high school. Crossing over the Georgia/Florida border to the mall in Jacksonville, Florida was the thing to do, since there was no mall in the military town where we resided. The biggest retailer in our military town was Walmart, so going to the mall was a big deal! We had an awesome time, laughing and hanging out. Later, he asked if he could escort me to the wedding of one of the Church members. Wedding? I told him I had nothing to wear. Not to be deterred, he let me purchase something to wear; which in my 18 year old mind was the best thing ever! Afterwards, he took me on a shopping spree and bought me Church clothes; which was his way of saying he hoped to see me in Church more often.

As we dated, or as my grandparents said "courted," my problems became his problems and his needs became my needs. I began to fall in love with his mind, ambitions, thoughts, goals and dreams. I was comfortable sharing my inner thoughts and secrets with him. He understood my "weirdness." He encouraged me to be creative and did not mind me being different. Even though I was a "babe in Christ" - meaning I was not as versed in the knowledge of Christ like the other Church girls he may have dated - he never judged me for it. In fact, every biblical question I raised he was able to answer and he took time to teach me the things I did not understand. He knew the Word of God inside and out, which made me want to learn more and have a closer relationship with God. He talked about God as if God was His all and I admired His relationship with God. As we were dating and falling in love, I did not see him as others saw him. To them he was a young, dynamic Minister who set the Church on fire with his God-given ability to deliver God's message with power and authority. I often heard the older saints say, "He is wise beyond his years." God gave Him a talent to teach, preach and articulate His Word in a way that everyone could understand - young and old. He was indeed blessed. People were beginning to rant and rave over his preaching style, but I saw beyond that...beyond the pulpit. God gave me the ability to see him from the inside out. He became my best friend. We would sit in his car, listening to all types of music, while looking at the stars, talking & daydreaming about the future. We would talk about anything and everything for hours. Some nights we did not even talk. We would just sit in silence, looking at the stars, while listening to the sounds of the crickets and the night. We became inseparable.

Since I moved around a lot, I had to grow up at a faster pace than most of my friends. Although I was young in age, I was more mature mentally than a lot of my friends. My husband was mentally mature, too. He had experienced a lot growing up, as well. We were able to relate to each other on another level. So, when he asked me to marry him, with no hesitation, I said YES! Noticing how inseparable we were, it seemed as if everyone around us knew we would eventually get married, but some of our friends were shocked - especially because of our ages. I was 19 years old and he was 21 years old, but we did not care.

Some older friends asked him, "Why are you marrying her, she hardly comes to Church? Mr. & Mrs. So & So's daughter may be a better fit for you! Unlike her, she is in Church EVERY Sunday."

Some of my friends were asking me, "Why are you marrying him, he's a preacher! Are you crazy? You want to marry a preacher? Girl… you won't be able to go to any clubs when you turn 21. You won't be able to hang out."

It is funny that years later some of the same people who told him not to marry me also told him they wish they had a wife like me. Also, some of the same people who told me I should not get married and should be having fun, hanging out in clubs with them, called me years later asking if he had any relatives they could talk to, now that their baby fathers were not any good for them. At the time, we did not care what people had to say. We were in love. I did not see myself as marrying a Minister, I saw myself as marrying my best friend. It was not until the day after our wedding that my life changed forever!

Since my future husband's family was traveling from up North for the wedding, my beloved grandfather - our Pastor - thought it was the perfect time to ordain my Minister future husband as a Reverend. My grandfather fondly called my future husband "his Joshua," while referring to himself as Moses. He loved my future husband like a son.

My family also welcomed my future husband with open arms. I fell in love with my future husband's family, especially his mother. To both families, having his Ordination Service on the day after our wedding was a great idea. His family would be able to witness both grand events. Everything was going as planned and I was super excited about both days. I was marrying the love of my life! Our ages did not stand in the way. The opinions from others did not bother us one bit. The love and bond we shared for each other were immeasurable. We were so excited about our future! As our wedding day drew closer, my excitement turned into worry.

One week before the service, my 1st Lady grandmother said to me, "You know you have to wear all white and sit in the two chairs in front of the Church on Sunday during the Ordination Service?"

Huh? What? No, Ma'am…I did not know! I was thinking to myself, she cannot be serious…white? I hated wearing white with a passion! At the time I did not own anything white, other than the wedding dress my mom was making for me to wear the following week.

"Sit in front of the Church, grandma? I have to sit in the very front?"

"Yes," she said. "That's what happens at an Ordination Service." She went on to explain, "It will be just you two sitting in the front. The Minsters, Deacons, Deaconess and Mother's Board are going to lay hands on you and your husband and then pray over the two of you. Oh, and you need a white hat, too."

"Hat? Noooo! I do not want to wear hats!"

"You are going to be a Minister's Wife now. You need lots of white dresses, hats, slips and white stockings."

My eyes bugged out of my head! White stockings? WHITE STOCKINGS! I was thinking to myself, now she is talking crazy! I am not wearing any white stockings! I have never volunteered to wear white stockings in my life! If you came across a picture of me in white stockings, my momma must have put them on me!

My grandmother continued, "Also, you need to get ready because, now that you are going to be his wife, they are going to ask you to introduce him when he travels to different Churches to preach."

I replied, "WHAT?? Ask me? Introduce who? Him? For what? No...I don't know him like that! Not to be introducing him! What am I supposed to say?"

Haahaaa...my Grandma started laughing so hard tears were coming out of her eyes! She said, "What do you mean you don't know him like that, you're marrying him 'ain't' you? Well I suggest you better get to know him! Welcome to my world, child...This is another world! You haven't seen anything yet! You will get the hang of it sooner or later."

As she continued to laugh like I had never heard her laugh before, she walked off into her closet to find me a white hat – while I stood in shock. At that moment, I think the scales I had on my eyes fell off and hit the floor! It was one of those moments when you realize that life as you had known it would never be the same. I once was blind, but now I really see! At the time, I could only think what am I getting myself into?

My grandmother was right - being a Minister's Wife was another world! How did I not realize the world I was about to enter into came attached to the man I was marrying. I was not groomed for the role. I did not grow up with people telling me I was going to marry a preacher. I was not prepared for the position! In my mind, I was just marrying my best friend who by the way happened to be a Minister. I realized on Saturday, July 3rd, 1999 I married my best friend, but on Sunday, July 4th I married the Church.

Hello, Babies!

In October of 2000, we welcomed into the world our first born child. In our eyes, she was perfect in every single way! I experienced a new found love that I am sure every mother experiences when she delivers her first child. She gave me an unexplainable joy and purpose! I was no longer living for myself. Everything within me changed. She was a blessing to us more than anyone would ever know! In fact, many people did not know 3 months before she was conceived, we found out we were pregnant with our first baby. We were so surprised and excited! We were not expecting to become pregnant so soon after marriage. At my monthly checkup, the nurse suddenly stopped performing the ultrasound. She said, "I'll be right back." I did not think anything of it until my doctor came in with a worried look on his face and continued with the ultrasound. Then, he asked me a series of questions as he was performing the ultrasound. At the time, my husband and I had confused looks on our faces.

The doctor said, "I am sorry to have to tell you this, but your baby does not have a heartbeat."

I exclaimed, "No heartbeat? I don't understand. What are you telling me? Are you saying my baby has died?"

He said, "Yes. I am so sorry."

As the doctor was talking, I blacked out in my mind! How is this possible? My baby died? Noooo! Not my baby! I remember my husband telling me, "It was going to be okay. We can have another baby in time. God will bless us with another one." I could tell in his voice that he was hurt, too. I tried my best to hold in what I was feeling inside. I literally wanted to jump off the exam table and run out the room! Instead, I just lied on the exam table, with tears running down my face, as my husband held my hand. The doctor told us he would schedule a D & C in the morning. So to make matters worse, I had to walk around until the next morning with a lifeless baby inside of me. Just the thought of that caused something deep within me mentally to die that day. Until this day, I cannot describe what I felt in words. Just the thought of having life in me one minute, then having to walk around with death in me the next, took a toll on my thoughts. At the time, it was hard for my young mind to process. Since I was a private person, I rarely confided in anyone outside of my husband. I did not tell him my true feelings, because I thought there was no way he could possibly understand. So, I kept the feelings of guilt and thinking it was somehow my fault, to myself. My husband gave me a lot encouraging words that I did not want to hear at the time. He told me we could have another child, but at the time I did not want another child! I wanted our baby's heartbeat back! I was hurt and angry with myself. Maybe I did not eat the correct fruit or veggies. Maybe I was taking my vitamins at the wrong time of the day. I was so confused and devastated, but felt I could not let anyone know. That was the first time I picked up and put on what I call my multi-mask. It was my ability to put on a facade of strength and courage when I was really feeling weak and vulnerable. It was my ability to hide the ugliness of pain behind a beautiful smile. I was suffering in silence and the people around me had no clue whatsoever…including my husband!

I can remember hearing my family and friends commending me for being strong. On the outside I was strong, but on the inside I was the total opposite. I hid my true feelings behind my multi-mask. By that time, I knew the "Church Talk." You know, the things we say when we want people to think we are a "Super Christian."

What is a Super Christian? I am glad you asked! You know, the Christians that have it all together...all the time? Nothing seems to bother them. The ones pretending that everything is perfect and every day is "Sunday" in their lives, when in reality they have some: Messed-up Mondays, Terrible Tuesdays, Weak Wednesdays, Troubled Thursdays, Frustrated Fridays and Sleepless Saturdays they hide from everyone. I remember telling someone it was God's will and I truly understood it was not in His plan for me to have a baby at the time, when really deep down inside I did not understand at all! How was this possible? Was not I supposed to understand God's will? Looking back at that time period, I never properly mourned. I did not give myself time to heal mentally, which I really should have done. I should have sought some outside counsel. I was too busy trying to impress and prove my strength to others. The truth of the matter was, regardless of how many months I had been pregnant, I still had lost my baby. I blamed myself for it.

I believe God heard my secret cry. He did not allow me to dwell in my self-pity for too long. Two months after losing the baby, I was pregnant again. I was so excited! I was extremely thankful and blessed that God had mercy on me! He saw what the others around me could not see - my silent tears. It was during that time period that I began to develop a closer relationship with the Lord. I was learning to trust Him. After a very difficult labor and delivery, we welcomed our first born daughter. What a joy to my soul!

Becoming A 1ˢᵗ Lady

Someone once told me that the first five years of marriage are the toughest years. I call them the learning years. It is during these years that you learn the most about each other. Since we married young, we were still trying to learn ourselves as well as each other. Due to my husband being in the military, he was only home roughly half of the year. Trying to balance a marriage to a Minister & submariner, motherhood, as well as my own goals and dreams proved to be challenging. We found a way to work as a team and made the best out of everything. While my husband was out to sea, I focused my time and energy on our daughter. I began to work fewer hours, so I could be her first teacher. It was a sacrifice we both were willing to make. We were blessed to have her and I wanted to give her the best of me. Until this day, I believe it was one of the best decisions I have made in my life. Being present to witness all of her "firsts" was priceless. She was a very intelligent and happy baby; a true blessing indeed! I thought I was a professional at the motherhood thing. I took pride in being a wife and mother.

Everything was falling into place as my husband was beginning his Shore Duty. Shore Duty meant my husband would not go back out to sea on a submarine for another 3 years. We were exceedingly excited, because although we had been married for some time, we had yet to spend a full year of married life together, because every 3 months my husband was traveling out to sea. It was during his Shore Duty that my grandfather got a phone call about a Church that was looking for a Senior Pastor. He thought my husband would be perfect for the Church. Although my husband was young, my grandfather knew he was well prepared for the task of being a full-time Senior Pastor of the particular Church. I, on the other hand, was not expecting it to happen so soon. Just when I was getting the hang of being a Minister's Wife, I was now about to be a "1st Lady" - like my Grandmother - to a group of people that I did not even know.

I will never forget entering into the historic Church for the first time. It was a gloomy day. Everyone looked down and out...for a reason. The former Senior Pastor had left the Church and took half the membership with him. It was terrible! Families who had basically grown up together were now turned against each other. I had never experienced anything like that and I am fairly sure my husband had not, as well. I was used to walking into a Church and feeling an uplifting Spirit upon entering the doors. I was used to being greeted with smiling faces. Going through the doors of that Church, on that particular Sunday, was like walking into a room of dark clouds, filled with doom and gloom. It was just sad.

I was exceptionally nervous for my husband to preach. I had never been so nervous in Church in my life! Well, let me take that back. There was one time my best friend's mother caught the Holy Ghost and felt compelled to testify about all my best friend's business. I was hoping and praying to God that her mother would not mention my name, too! Whew! But, even that time could not nearly compare to the nervousness I was feeling on that day. I realized we were "not in Kansas anymore." It was different. Those people were hurting and needed a Word from the Lord to get understanding of what was happening. Families were against families and friends were against friends. That day, God used my husband in a mighty way! The words God gave him for the people were so powerful and profound you could actually feel the switch in the atmosphere. People began to cry. When I say cry, I am talking about long, drawn out war cries! People all over the Church were shouting! It was as if they were trying to wash away all the clouds of doom and gloom with their tears. The Holy Spirit took over the service. You could actually see burdens being lifted from the faces of the people. I had never been more proud of my husband. I witnessed with my own eyes how he allowed God to use him to help deliver and comfort His people from the pain and confusion they were experiencing. Prior to leaving the Church, one of the oldest Mothers, who was a well-respected member of the Church and community, came up to me and said, "Your husband is going to be our next Senior Pastor." She stated God had revealed it to her. Wow! I was speechless! When we got in the car headed home, my husband said God revealed to him that he was going to be the next Senior Pastor of the Church. I remember, together, we began to pray about it and sure enough, at the age of 23, my husband was called to become the Senior Pastor of the historic Church. At the time, he was the youngest Senior Pastor in Southeast Georgia. During that time, I had been studying my grandmother and preparing myself for the duties of a 1st Lady. My grandmother was not one of those 1st Ladies who just sat on the front row and looked pretty. Although, she would give you a run for your money with her designer dresses, hats, purses and shoes - she believed in giving her time, talents and treasures back to the Lord. You could find my grandmother working diligently on a given Church committee, on any given day. Whether it was cooking, teaching, putting together fundraising programs, etc., she did all she could to edify the Church. She was even the Church secretary. I knew when the time arrived, I wanted to be a 1st Lady who worked in the Church like my grandmother.

The first couple of months as the "First Family" were a little rough, due to the fact we all were starting at ground zero. After the Church was split, my husband literary had to rebuild every ministry and auxiliary in the Church. A lot of the ministry leaders had left with the former Senior Pastor. To make matters even more awkward, the former Senior Pastor started a Church down the street from our Church. It felt as if we were in the middle of a perfect storm. All eyes were on my young husband. There were some people who wished us the best and there were some people who hoped we were going to fail. I was reminded of the days when we used to sit in the car, looking up at the stars and dreaming of our future. The only thing my husband ever said he wanted was to be a Senior Pastor. In fact, his goal was to leave the Navy and pastor full-time. Ironically, God did not wait for my husband to leave the Navy to become a Senior Pastor, God made it possible while he was still in the Navy. I started to see God in another light. I was learning the power of words and speaking things into existence. I was truly discovering another level within my faith.

I started working in the Church for the first time. At the time, everyone in the Church was on one accord. We were all determined to prove the naysayers wrong. Everyone began to step up to the plate and do what needed to be done to restore the Church again. Like my grandmother, I wanted to do my part. I became a Sunday School teacher for one of the Youth Sunday School classes. Me? The person who used to skip Sunday School classes at my grandfather's Church? The one who hid in the bathroom and between the small space of the old Church and the new Church until Sunday school was over? I was so thankful it was a small class at first, and I absolutely loved the children that were in the class. As I was teaching, I was also learning. It was during that time that I developed a strong desire to do God's will by using my talents within the Church. The Sunday School class opened the door for God to us me to start teaching Youth Bible Study. I went on to develop a Youth Department, as well as organize community youth events. God also led me to establish a Nursing Home ministry.

There was a huge growth boom within the Church. The anointing of the Lord was heavy on my husband, as well as me. We were living our motto: "Changing Lives through Jesus Christ." The Church was growing and the people were prospering. So much so that under my husband's administration, the Church completed a half million dollar renovation - all new everything! God used us to bring life again into the Church. It was a growing period for both of us. It was at that point God started to give me dreams again. I used to have detailed dreams as a child, but I would wake up confused. I never understood them; they did not make sense to me. I also used to see visions that no one around me could explain; so I stopped telling people what I saw, because it would scare them. As an adult, I would have dreams and some of the things that were in my dreams would manifest. Just like as a child, I never really told anyone. I would mention it to certain people, but I never went into enough details for them to start asking me questions. One night I dreamt of a Women's Conference. In the dream I was actually at a Women's Conference in our Church. It was so powerful that when I woke up out of my dream, I had to write down everything so that I would not forget it. One of the Church members I was working closely with on a youth project, called me the day after my dream. I felt led to explain my dream to her. She was impressed and said I should host a Women's Conference, and she even volunteered to help me. After talking to my Husband about a Women's Conference, I took all my ideas to the next Women's Ministry meeting and they shot them down - every last one of my ideas! They said, "That has never been done before. People around here don't support events like that, and furthermore it's not in the Women's Ministry budget."

I left the meeting feeling confused and defeated. After talking to the Church member I shared my dream with, we took it upon ourselves to make the Women's Conference happen in spite of what was said in the Women's Ministry meeting. She believed in my dream so much that she and her family started purchasing items and supplies. With the Pastor's approval, we began to turn my vision into a reality. Soon other women of the Church asked if they could assist. It was not long before all the women of the Church, young and old, got on one accord and were onboard with the vision. The Women's Conference ended up being everything I could have imagined, plus more! The conference was beautiful! It really showed me the power of God. Until this day, the Women's Conference God gave me in a dream is still one of the greatest events in that area. I commend those who are keeping my God-given dream alive, years later. The Women's Conference taught me I have the power to turn my dreams and visions into reality. God did not only give me the vision, but he also gave me the provision. He sent the right people with the right resources to help with the vision. The Women's Conference also showed me no man or woman could stop what God had already ordained. Just because others could not see the vision, did not mean it was not real. Just because it had not been done before, did not mean that it could not be done. God did not give the vision to them, He gave it to me. In time, God slowly revealed it to them. We all came on one accord and a beautiful blessing was birthed, that I pray will continue to soar and outlive me.

Come Out Of The Closet

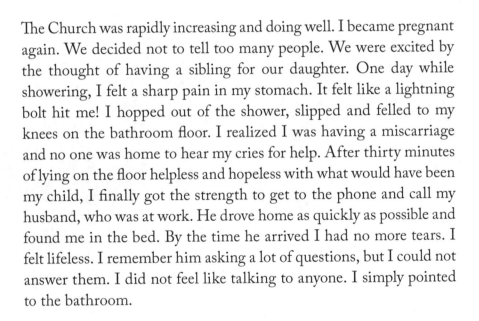

The Church was rapidly increasing and doing well. I became pregnant again. We decided not to tell too many people. We were excited by the thought of having a sibling for our daughter. One day while showering, I felt a sharp pain in my stomach. It felt like a lightning bolt hit me! I hopped out of the shower, slipped and felled to my knees on the bathroom floor. I realized I was having a miscarriage and no one was home to hear my cries for help. After thirty minutes of lying on the floor helpless and hopeless with what would have been my child, I finally got the strength to get to the phone and call my husband, who was at work. He drove home as quickly as possible and found me in the bed. By the time he arrived I had no more tears. I felt lifeless. I remember him asking a lot of questions, but I could not answer them. I did not feel like talking to anyone. I simply pointed to the bathroom.

He entered the bathroom and exclaimed, "JESUS," as he saw our child's small fetus lying on the bathroom floor. I cannot remember what else he said, but I remember him telling me I needed to go to the hospital.

I yelled at him saying, "No! I am not going anywhere! Our baby is dead! There is nothing they can do! I'll go to my doctor in the morning! Leave me alone, please!"

He left me alone and proceeded to clean up the bathroom, as I lied in the bed until the next morning and cried until there were no more tears left inside of me. The next day, it was time to put on my multi-mask again. I lied on the exam table, waiting on the same doctor who told me that our first child had died inside of me.

The doctor confirmed what I already knew by saying, "Your womb is empty."

He looked at me with sadness in his eyes and asked me to explain the graphic details of my miscarriage. He kept asking me if I was okay.

With my multi-mask on I said, "Yes, it was God's will."

He told me to take care of myself. But, I will never forget the worried look he had in his eyes. That day, another piece of me died mentally.

Over the next few weeks I became depressed. No one was used to seeing me in a depressed state. I started missing a lot of Church events. I just wanted to stay in the bed. My husband and I began to argue over small things. I became distanced. Looking back, I believe I was probably suffering from post-partum depression. Neither of us knew the symptoms of post-partum depression. At the time, I had never heard of it - but I knew something was terribly wrong with me. I would get so down some days that all I wanted to do was be alone in the dark. Since our house had a lot of windows, I found comfort within the darkness of our bedroom closet. I would sit in our bedroom closet for hours, alone in the dark. The darkness in the closet was so thick somedays, I felt like it was choking me. My husband did not understand what was going on with me so he did not tell anyone. To keep the peace, he would just let me go into the closet. There were times when death would cross my mind.

One day, while sitting in the closet, my daughter banged on the door and began yelling, "Mommy!" I started to weep as she was crying, trying to open the door. I was too weak mentally to open the door, although my heart wanted to open it. She stopped crying, and sat down on the other side door. I could hear her breathing. We both sat with our backs up against the door for what felt like 2 hours. All of a sudden she commenced to sing a song that I had sung to her ever since she was in my womb. Her angelic voice sang, "This little light of mine, I'm going to let it shine." The more she sang, the more I regained my strength. She began singing louder and louder. I had never heard her sing that loudly and clearly before! I slowly turned around. When I turned around I saw light coming from under the door, as well as my daughter's hand trying to reach under the crack of the door. I grabbed her small fingers, as her little voice sang the song as loudly as she could possibly sing it. I felt a peaceful Spirit come over me, and at that moment I knew it was time for me to come out of the darkness. I slowly turned the door knob and my baby girl was standing there looking like an angel. She yelled, "Mommy! Mommy!" I quickly hugged her and held her tightly, for at least 15 minutes. God used my daughter to deliver me out of the darkness, into the light. On that day, I promised God, my child and myself that no matter how bad things became, I would never allow myself to become that down and out and I would never enter into a dark closet again. I vowed to never find comfort in darkness and to always seek the light. God showed me that although I had lost two babies, I still had a beautiful little girl to live for! I still had a purpose! She needed me just as much as I needed her!

Seasons Change

Everything was well with the Church for a couple of years. Things started to change after I found out I was pregnant again. This time, I was mentally prepared for anything and knew if it was the Lord's will that I would deliver a child. I now understood that children were a blessing from God. He had the ultimate right to give and to take away. I was not in a position to question God and I was now at peace with God and fully trusted Him. I was excited when I found out I was having a boy. Because of my troubled pregnancy history, I was put on bedrest extremely early. I began speaking life and visualizing my son playing and crawling; although he was not born yet. My husband was enormously excited, too! We tried to come up with a name for our son. My husband wanted to name our son after one of the youngest kings in the Bible. I did not want to choose that name because we already had a little boy at our Church with the same name. I wanted to name our son Malachi, because I felt God had opened up a window and poured me out another blessing. We went back and forth until we both agreed to name our son after my husband.

The Church members seemed to have become complacent and did not want to grow anymore. They were no longer following the vision my husband had outlined for the Church. They were doing what was right in their own eyes. It was as if God had purposefully hardened their hearts. We could not understand what was transpiring. The timing was horrible, because my husband decided to step out on faith and leave the military to pastor full-time. The Church had "promised" to take care of our family if he left the military. Once he was honorably discharged from the military, the Church reneged on those promises.

Since I was pregnant, I did not want to add the stress of the Church onto my worries - so I did not. I had learned to turn it over to God. We were confused. We needed answers and the only one that could give it to us was the Lord. It was not unusual to find us at the Church at 2am or 3am, with our daughter in tow. We would be at the altar praying, praising or just meditating. We were seeking the Lord. We wanted understanding from Him. We were not going to stop until He answered us! After a couple of weeks of fasting, praying and petitioning, God responded to our prayers. One of my husband's friends' home Church needed a Senior Pastor. My husband's friend, who was also a Senior Pastor, called to tell my husband to submit his resume. The Church was in a small town near Augusta, GA. Maybe this was the answer to our prayers; we weren't sure. We were walking by faith and had the mindset that if it was the Lord's will, it would happen.

My husband and I went to visit the Church prior to the Church calling him to preach. When I say it was in the country...it was in the country! Both of us being from the city were looking around at the scenery as if we had landed on another planet. When we pulled up to the Church, no one was there, which was a good thing. We did not want anyone seeing us and asking questions. We were on a spy mission. We wanted to check out the area. Since it was three and a half hours from where we resided, we wanted to make sure it was worth leaving our current Church. There was nothing special about the outside of the Church. It looked like a typical country Church. I remember my husband asking why on earth his friend would recommend him for that Church. My husband went on to say, "I'm just going to keep my obligation to preach and that's it. There's no way I'm leaving our Church to come to this Church. After all the building and hard work we've invested with our Church, this Church would be a step backwards." Feeling a little disappointed, he still kept the arrangement to preach at this Church as scheduled.

The morning he was scheduled to preach at the country Church, I was so nervous that I did not know I had turned the iron up too high, and burned my skirt. Sadly, it was the only church outfit I had brought and there was not time to purchase another outfit. My husband assured me I looked fine. Upon entering the doors of the Church, I was greeted with so much love that it felt overwhelming; so much so that I had totally forgotten I had an iron print on my black skirt! It was a different Spirit in the Church. As I sat down, more and more people shuffled through the doors. They all had looks on their faces that said they were truly happy to be in the house of the Lord. It was a completely different atmosphere than when we first went to our current Church. The Spirit in the service was so high, that I knew my husband was going to let God use him in a powerful and profound way. My husband lived for those types of moments. And sure enough, my husband preached like he had never preached before! He was in his element. We had, as the old Saints would say, "A shouting good time!" It felt as if my husband was already their Senior Pastor. The country Church felt like home. When we got in the car on the way back home, we both said, "This is it!" Neither one of us could get a word in edgewise! We were talking over each other and so excited about everything that had transpired at the Church - from Sunday School, to the Deacons' devotion, to the choir. The choir was AWESOME! It is rare to find a choir filled with lead singers. Everyone that touched the microphone could outright blow! This was it!

We both wanted to move on from our current Church; we had truly outgrown it. Our work was complete. God had allowed my husband to accomplish a lot of Kingdom building under his administration. The Church's morale had been rebuilt after the split, new members had been added, and a huge renovation had taken place, not to mention we were one of the first Churches in the area with an industrial-sized elevator. Furthermore, God had used me to start a Women's Conference and Youth Department/youth community events, as well as a Nursing Home Ministry. We had planted the seeds and it was time for someone else to water them.

Our faith went into overdrive. We believed we were going to be the next First Family of the country Church, outside of Augusta, GA. I believed so much that I thought it was a good idea to start looking for a house in the Augusta area; although the country Church had not even decided on their next Senior Pastor yet. So, we started researching the area and found a house that fit our needs. We became preapproved for the house without anyone's knowledge. I started packing up our current house; I only left out the essentials. Although we had not been "called" to the Church yet, I had enough faith to believe it was ours so I started to prepare myself for the move. My family thought I had lost my mind when they came over and saw our house packed and ready to move. We were literally living out of boxes! I had so much faith that God would call us to the country Church, that I wanted to have everything in place before it was time for me to have Jr.

It was time for Jr. to be born. I was so excited! My normal doctor was not available so his assistant, whom I had grown fond of, was present to deliver our son. After hours and hours of labor, it was clear that something was going wrong. I heard the nurse say Jr.'s heartbeat rate and oxygen levels were going up and down. I had no idea what she was referencing. I remember my mother started to pray aloud. After delivering our son, I could hear the doctor saying, "Come on baby breathe. Breathe!" Our son's face was blue and he was unresponsive. We came to find out his umbilical cord had wrapped around his neck 3 times! As I was pushing, the umbilical cord was choking him, causing him not to be able to breathe. I remember my husband, mother and nurses started to speak life into our son, as the doctor tried to get him to breathe. All of a sudden our son began to cry and everyone in the room praised the Lord - including the doctor and nurses. As I look back at the time period, I cannot help but to thank God, because it could have been worse!

A couple of months after the birth of our son, the country Church called my husband to be their next Senior Pastor. We had to say goodbye to our current Church, which was not easy. It did not make sense to leave in the eyes of others. Why go to a smaller Church when we had invested so much time and energy into the Church we were leaving. In my opinion, God had allowed us to take them as far as they were willing to go and grow. It is always difficult when leaving a Church. Some of the Church members become like family. I often wondered what my life would be like if we would have remained. Then, I stopped wondering and started thanking God for all the good things that transpired while I was at our first Church. Without being at that Church, I would not have become as committed to the cause of Christ. I learned to wholly trust and love Jesus. During our first pastorate, God allowed me to discover hidden talents. During our first pastorate, I grew as a Christian and utilized my gifts. My faith became immeasurable! I also learned to appreciate the Church and the people within it. I am very thankful for the good times and learned lessons from the bad times. I will always have love for our first Church family. They will forever be a part of my testimony and dwell within my heart!

New Beginnings!

Our new Church family welcomed us with opened arms. Here I was again "the new girl" - or should I say "new lady" - in a town where I had no family or friends, outside of my husband and children. It took a moment to adjust. I had always had a support system back home, with my father and mother, and this was the first time I did not have any family or friends to lean on. At the time, our son was only a couple of months old and I had trust issues when it came to my children. I did not like people touching or holding them; especially with them being so young. In the beginning, I think I offended some of the Church members. They would ask if they could hold him and I would say, "No." Some of the Church members called me mean, but I did not care. They would not be the ones up with him at 3am, due to him having a virus or cold given to him by a Church member.

When a 1st Lady has a baby, it is like the Church has a baby. In the Church members' eyes, the baby belongs to them, too. The baby becomes a part of their lives. They become protective of the child. It was something I became accustomed to as a Pastor's granddaughter. Some members always wanted to know every single detail about our children, so they can be the first to tell the other members. Conversely, it was good to know my children had people always concerned about them and praying for them. I established boundaries early on, and only let a couple of people, who I felt comfortable with, help with my children. The Church members respected my decision of not wanting my children passed all around the Church, and all became well.

The new Church was growing at such as fast pace! People were joining left and right; there was literally nowhere to sit! People were everywhere, young and old. It was a fire hazard! People would stand against the sanctuary walls, all service, just to hear a Word from the Lord from the powerful "new preacher" God had sent. I had never seen that many people hungry for the Word! There were people in all of the classrooms viewing the service, and the overflow areas were maxed to capacity. I could not keep up with all the names and faces. Each Sunday people were joining the Church. My husband and I were exceptionally excited. God had opened up the flood gates of Heaven and poured us out a blessing!

We were on a mission to "Change Lives through Jesus Christ." Since we were new in town, my husband had to establish relationships with the community and other Senior Pastors and Churches. We had a mutual understanding that the relationship-building had to take place. He went to as many events as possible to show his support. We knew in order for people to support our events, we had to support their events. My husband's relationship-building and dynamic preaching led to him becoming a highly sought after Preacher. He was booking preaching/speaking engagements left and right - revivals, Church Anniversaries, community events…you name it. God was using my husband in a meaningful and mighty way! I was very proud of him and all the things he was accomplishing and achieving. I was behind him 100 percent, and did my part in understanding he was not going to be home as much as he used to be home. It was fine because we are building up God's Kingdom, as well as establishing our future. Although my husband was often gone doing the work of the Lord, I never complained one time because I was able to see the bigger picture. Lives were being changed for the better and who was I to stand between him and God?

I was asked to become the Youth Director at the Church once the person who held the position decided to retire. I gladly accepted the position. Unknowingly, God had already trained me and prepared me for the role at our last Church. I was placed over everything pertaining to the young people in the Youth Department, which was a big task because there were lots of children and youth and many youth groups and events throughout the year. I was thankful for the staff and youth leaders who took my vision for the Youth Department and ran with it. Although I was younger and did not have all the degrees that some of the people under me possessed, God gave me an anointing and a passion for youth that was unexplainable. The youth leaders understood my passion and anointing and we were able to accomplish amazing things for Christ. The Church was growing in every area. God was using me and my husband in an extraordinary manner to help build His Kingdom.

Break Time!

Things were going well for the first couple of years at our new Church home. God was being glorified and lives were being changed for the better. My husband was not only getting recognition within the state, but nationwide. He was chosen as one of America's favorite Pastors in a nationwide magazine. I was so proud of him! Things were going well for me, also. As Youth Director, I was so happy, because we had an overflow of children that were on fire for the Lord. God used me to create programs and events the youth wanted to participate in and enjoyed. Before I would arrive at the Church, there would always be tons of youth waiting on me. It brought joy to my heart and soul knowing the youth could be anywhere doing anything, but they wanted to be at Church. Even the ones that most would have labeled "troubled youth" (I called them "misunderstood") were active participants.

It is always a joy to introduce Jesus to youth on a level they can understand Him, and inspire them to want to learn more about Him. Sadly, some leaders are so "deep" with their teaching that their teaching can only be understood by themselves and the Lord. Oftentimes, Jesus taught in parables. If it is not broken, and it worked for Jesus, why fix it? With youth, you are either a hit or a miss. There is no in between. They either like you or they do not. If they do not like you, they will tell you through their actions. They will either participate or they will not.

I was grateful for the youth God entrusted in my care. I loved each one like they were my own child. They gave me joy and a purpose. I looked forward to helping them fall in love with Jesus. It seemed as if both my husband and my dreams were coming true. All the hard work and sacrifices we made were paying off in major ways! We were being blessed beyond measure! We were conquering a foreign land…together! He was walking in his purpose and so was I! Our will for our lives matched God's will for our lives!

Times began to change when I found out I was pregnant. Yes… again. The pregnancy was unexpected, but I was excited. This pregnancy was different than the rest. My husband was very busy throughout my entire pregnancy. So much so that I often found myself going to checkups and doctor visits alone. Before, he was always present with me at the visits. This time, it was an inconvenience to his schedule. I tried to be an "understanding wife" and did not express to him that I missed him going to the doctor visits with me. I was beginning to feel a disconnection from my husband. Here I was excited about the baby, and he was busy with the work of the Lord. I did not want it to seem as if I was jealous of him doing what he was called to do, but during that time I felt alone. I also started to feel homesick. Yes, I had my Church family, but this was the first time I had to go through a pregnancy without my immediate family. At that point, it was clear that Church and the work of the Church were first in our marriage and lives. Even pregnancy did not change that fact. After an emergency C-section, we welcomed into the world a beautiful baby girl. Seeing my husband hold her for the first time brought tears to my eyes and joy to my heart. He adored her! She was another beautiful addition to our family!

After the birth of our daughter, I decided to take some time off from my Church duties, and delegated my responsibilities to the youth leaders in my department. Everyone worked as a team and the Youth Department was still prospering and growing in my absence. During that time, my husband was becoming even busier.

Every week he had a different preaching/speaking engagement; he was constantly traveling. There were a lot of late nights and early mornings. It seemed like he accepted every preaching engagement he was offered; from the smallest events to the largest events! My husband was traveling from city to city and state to state – all week long. He would literally be so drained some Sundays that he would come home to quickly rest up before his next engagement. At that point, it was becoming overwhelming for me and I decided not to go with him to some of his engagements. It was important to me to take time off to spend with our newborn and children. My husband became disappointed with me when I would tell him I did not want to go to his preaching engagements. I had just birthed a baby and I was tired. We would argue about my absence, but I knew a lot of big events were coming up and I needed to rest my mind and body. I needed balance. He needed balance, too. In my opinion too much of anything is never good…including Church! He understood my choice; so I thought!

After about two months of a much needed break, after having our second daughter, I returned to Church and everyone was ecstatic I was back. While away, I was able to plan the first Fall Festival for the Youth Department. I decided to go all out with a Noah's Ark theme. There were games, inflatables, wagon rides, petting zoo etc. It was a great time for the Church and the community. I was extremely busy the day of the Fall Festival. In fact, anytime I plan an event I rarely get to enjoy it. I like to work and go all out as if it is my last time planning an event. I am generally busy making sure everyone else has smiling faces. Later, I go back and look at pictures or videos just to see where I can approve in making the next event better.

To my surprise, I did not know that event was going to change my life forever. I remember the scene like it was yesterday. I was walking with my hands filled with items, to take inside of the kitchen door of the Church. There were two church members standing at the door having a conversation.

One of the ladies said to the other, "Ughhh…What is *she* doing here?"

I turned around to see who she was referencing. I saw a "woman," I had never seen before standing by the jumping inflatables. She was talking to one of the men of the Church, who happened to be the husband of one of my youth leader's. The woman and my youth leader's husband were laughing and giggling; they were having what appeared to be a pleasant conversation.

The other lady who was standing at the door said, "She is out here to get somebody's husband."

I stopped what I was doing and looked at both of the ladies. I decided to keep walking into the kitchen, because I never entertained Church gossip. I still remember the look in the lady's eyes after she said, "She is out here to get somebody's husband."

At the time I did not think much of the conversation, but as I reflect, she had the demeanor of a person who knew something, but did not want to be the person to tell it. She gazed directly at me when she said, "She is out her to get somebody's husband." But my mind was focused on Church work; besides I knew she could not possibly be talking about my husband. So, that conversation was none of my business and I wanted no part of it. Soon after the Fall Festival, the strange woman joined the Church.

I'm Back!

After two months of being absent from Sunday morning services, it felt good to be back. There were even more new faces. One particular Sunday I was sitting where I usually sit in Church with my children and a little girl squeezed past me to sit next to our oldest daughter. I did not think anything of it until the little girl kept putting her feet on the pew in front of us. I fanned her foot down and told her with my eyes to "stop." Five minutes later, she did it again.

This time I said, "Stop! Do not put your foot on the pew again."

She smiled and returned to drawing on her Church program. After Church was over, I asked my oldest daughter who was the little girl, I had never seen before.

She responded, "Oh, that's my friend from school."

A couple of days later, I pulled into the Church parking lot at the same time as one of the Church members who always gave me items for my children. She was always very sweet and kind. She loved my children and would often surprise me with gifts for them.

She said, "Hi 1st Lady, let me introduce you to my grandchildren."

One of her grandchildren was the little girl who had been sitting next to my daughter in church. Her two brothers were with their grandmother, as well.

The Church member said, "I want them to become a part of the youth groups and activities."

I told her, "Sure! The more the merrier!"

One Sunday, not long after that encounter, I was walking towards the Pastor's Study and ran into my husband, the little girl and the woman who the ladies were gossiping about at the Fall Festival. They were all coming out of the New Members class. Our church was growing at such a rapid pace that New Members class was a requirement for the numerous people who were joining the Church. New Members class lasted for several weeks, and during that period the new members became familiar with the mission of the Church, as well as the Pastor. We all greeted each other and I welcomed them both to the Church.

The woman said to the little girl, "Tell her what you said to me this morning. Tell her!"

The little girl looked at her and said, "Nooooo." The little girl was truly embarrassed. She then started to hide behind the woman.

I had one of those confused smiles on my face.

The woman proceeded to tell me that her daughter said to her while they were getting ready for Church, "Mommy, your hair is so pretty. It looks like the 1st Lady's hair at the Church."

Shocked, my confused smile turned into a confused laugh. "Ha!" I said, "Aww…Ok. That's nice!"

The woman was smiling from ear to ear. My husband was standing in the hallway with a fake smile, too. I was thinking to myself, No, ma'am! Your hair doesn't look anything like mine…not even close! The only thing our hair had in common was that our part was on the same side of our heads. But I took the compliment for what it was; after which, we all proceeded to the Church service.

During the ride home from Church, I brought up the "caught off guard" moment I had with the woman. I said to my husband, laughing, "Babes, I am not sure about that woman's hair looking like mine." We both laughed and he said she told him that in New Member's class earlier. He thought it was strange that she would mention that to him during class. He said there is clearly no comparison. I said yes, it was a little strange and awkward. We both laughed it off.

A couple of weeks went by and my husband came to me saying, "Do you remember that little girl that asked about your hair? I saw her and her mother at the store. They were on their way to cheerleading practice and she asked does our oldest daughter cheer? I told her she used to cheer before we moved here. She said they have spots on the cheer team her daughter cheers on." My husband went on to say she asked for our phone number and he gave her our house number so she could tell me more. I told him at that time I am not interested in signing our daughter up for cheering because of all the Church activities she is a part of - thanks, but no thanks. The day after the conversation with my husband, the woman called me saying her daughter really liked my daughter and wanted to know if my daughter could come over her house to spend the night and play. I informed her, "No, I do not allow my daughter to spend the night at other people's house I do not know." I was thinking to myself, everyone at Church knows how I feel about my children, but it is obvious no one gave her the memo. She was trying to convince me she was a good person. She kept saying how her daughter really liked our daughter and how they were in the same grade and school. I politely told her no, again.

She called back the next week and my husband answered the phone. She wanted to know if our daughter could have a playdate at McDonalds with her daughter. I gave him "a look" and he said, "I do not see any harm in going to McDonald's. She does need to make friends and do things outside of Church activities. I really do not see the big deal. I'll take her if you want me to do it." I remember telling him, "You know I don't like someone trying to force something or themselves on me. I told her 'no thank you' the first time she called here. That's just strange." My husband said I was being overprotective and it was just a playdate at McDonald's. I thought well maybe I was being overprotective and overacting. It was not a house, it was just McDonald's play land with a Church member's child, and my husband did not see any harm in letting her go. Eventually, I agreed to him taking her that day. When they came back, my daughter was all smiles and said she had a great time.

One week, I decided to surprise my husband and go with him each night to a revival he was preaching in a nearby city. He was overjoyed the children and I were in attendance. This was the first revival I had attended since taking a much needed break, after having our third child. I was excited to be present to support my husband. The first night, I was asked to introduce him. As I rose to go to the podium, the entire Church started clapping, cheering and chanting "1st Lady." The overwhelming love caught me off guard! I saw the smiles and heard the cheering of our members. It was warm and loving. Those people had become my family and I loved them just as much as they loved me. They entrusted me with their children. It was at that moment I was remarkably proud to be the 1st Lady of that Church, and I was honored to introduce my husband. Service was great as usual. My husband allowed God to use him to preach with clarity and conviction!

After service, I saw the woman walking to her car - past a group of Church members. I spoke to the woman and the other Church members, but she did not speak back. She looked as if she had an attitude. I thought it was a little strange, but figured maybe she did not hear me speak to her. The woman was present for the next two nights of revival, but went out of her way to avoid me. Again, at the moment I thought it was a little strange, since she had been calling my house and darn near begging me to be her friend. Oh, well. I thought to myself, I never had a Church member go out of their way not to speak to me. What was her problem?

I did not dwell too much on the issue. Anyways, the revival was a success and it felt great to be able to support my husband and see God use him in an anointed manner, to help win souls for Christ.

Let's Take This Show On The Road

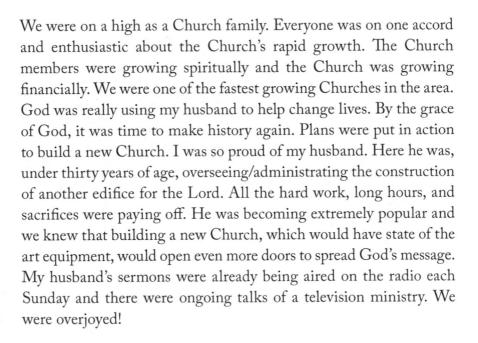

We were on a high as a Church family. Everyone was on one accord and enthusiastic about the Church's rapid growth. The Church members were growing spiritually and the Church was growing financially. We were one of the fastest growing Churches in the area. God was really using my husband to help change lives. By the grace of God, it was time to make history again. Plans were put in action to build a new Church. I was so proud of my husband. Here he was, under thirty years of age, overseeing/administrating the construction of another edifice for the Lord. All the hard work, long hours, and sacrifices were paying off. He was becoming extremely popular and we knew that building a new Church, which would have state of the art equipment, would open even more doors to spread God's message. My husband's sermons were already being aired on the radio each Sunday and there were ongoing talks of a television ministry. We were overjoyed!

Our ministry came full circle when my husband was invited back to the area we considered home, where our former Church was located, for two preaching engagements at two different Churches on the same Sunday. We were jubilant because it was our first time returning home since being called as the First Family of our current Church. We were extremely excited because our current Church members were coming, too! We took coach buses full of members on the road with us! It was a grand occasion. Many people had doubted we would be able to recapture the success we had with our first

Church. God proved them wrong, and everyone welcomed us back with open arms. The favor of the Lord was upon us!

A week before we were scheduled to travel back home, I lost my ATM card and was using my husband's card until a new card was mailed. One night after a late night preaching engagement, my husband called in a frantic state asking if I had his ATM card.

I replied, "Sorry, I forgot to place it back in your wallet."

He said, "WHAT!?! I am at the gas station and I am about to run out of gas!"

He was so upset, he hung up the phone on me. I tried to call him back, but he would not answer. One hour later, my husband arrived home and I asked what happened. He replied, "Thank God I ran into 'the woman' at the gas station. She gave me twenty dollars to get gas, so I could make it back home." I felt so bad because I knew my husband did not like to ask anyone for anything - especially a Church member!

The day of our homecoming celebration had arrived and everything was going well. It was an amazing feeling to be home and to show our current Church family the area where we used to live. That Sunday, my husband was on program to preach at two Churches; one for a morning service and one for an afternoon service. After the morning service, lunch was served.

While eating lunch my husband said, "There goes the woman that gave me the 20 dollars. I hate I had to borrow it from her. I want to give it back as soon as possible." He took 20 dollars from his wallet and asked could I go give it back to the woman, because she may need it.

I said, "Sure." I went over to the table where she was sitting alone and said, "Thank you so much for giving this to my husband the other day at the gas station."

She looked shocked that I was handing her back her 20 dollars. She did a fake smile and said, "No problem. You're welcome." Then, I returned to the head table where my husband and family were eating.

Everyone was ranting and raving about how well my husband had preached during the morning service. I happened to glance back over in the direction of where the woman was seated. She had an identical look on her face as she did the day she did not speak to me at revival. It was almost as if the woman had an attitude. After eating, it was time to travel to the next service and all the Church members loaded up in the coach buses. My husband and I were asked to take a family picture. As we were taking our family picture, I remember looking toward the buses and seeing the woman staring at us; she looked sad.

'Tis The Season!

The holidays were rapidly approaching and every auxiliary in the Church was planning their big Christmas event. In most Churches, Christmas and Easter are the busiest days of the year. It was the time to pay honor and tribute to our Savior - in every way possible. The one thing all our Church members had in common, regardless of gender, ethnicity, economic background or social status was our love for Jesus Christ. He was to be celebrated! Whether it was planning the Christmas program, Church member fellowship dinner, or auxiliaries Christmas parties, almost every leader in the Church was busy. I was tirelessly planning for the Youth Department's Christmas events. As such, I was in need of as many volunteers as possible! Children whom I had not seen all year showed up to participate in the Youth Department's Christmas events. I never turned a child away – even if the child had been missing in action from church all year. In my eyes, Easter and Christmas were the perfect times to introduce people to Christ. The Church is supposed to help bring people to Christ, not turn them away. Who was I to tell someone they could not participate in the celebration of Christ? There is always room!

This year, I was hoping a lot of parents would step up and help out. We were busting at the seams with children and youth wanting to participate in our different Youth events. I remember my assistant said to me, "You should ask the mom of those children who are standing over there if she can help with the Youth Department." I looked across the room and saw the woman talking to a Deacon.

My assistant went on to say the woman mentioned to her a couple of days ago she used to assist with the youth at her previous Church. My assistant also said the woman had recently joined the choir and had inquired about helping with the children's songs for the Christmas play. My assistant continued to say, she noticed the woman was always one of the first people at Church, every time there was an event or when Pastor was scheduled to preach at other events outside of the Church. She appeared to be eager and "on fire" for the Lord, so it wouldn't hurt to ask. My assistant knew we needed as many parents onboard as possible to help out.

It was not until my assistant mentioned it to me that I took notice that the woman was one of the first to arrive at Church. Some days she beat the Deacon in charge of opening the door; she would be sitting in the parking lot patiently waiting. Also, I noticed almost every time my husband would preach, "the Spirit" would hit her hard! She would fallout and "shout" all under the pew sometimes. The ushers often had to leave their posts to attend to her. I decided to ask the woman, as well as some of the other active parents in the Church, to come onboard to help with the Youth Department. When I approached the woman about volunteering she surprisingly said, "No. I don't think I have the time." I was puzzled at first because it seemed as if she had more time than me! Just as my assistant stated, she was always at Church. As a matter of fact, every time my husband preached she was present, but often without her children. It did not matter if he was preaching in another county or close city, she would be in attendance. At the time, I did not give it much thought. A lot of the Church members were faithful followers. All of the Church members loved the God-given sermons my husband preached. Some members never missed an engagement; they proudly supported their Pastor and Church events.

I remember telling my husband, I asked the woman to help out and she said, "No." That was a first for me. Up until that point, everyone I had asked in the Church to help me with anything, big or small, gladly accepted. As a matter of fact, they were happy I had asked them to participate. Working together gave me a chance to get to know the Church members better and it gave the Church members a chance to get to know me better. I never wanted to be an unapproachable 1st Lady. I started developing relationships with the Church members and I found myself pulling talents out of them. Many of the Church members discovered hidden talents and went on to do great things for the Church. As I was telling my husband about the conversation between the women and me, he gave me the same look he gave when I was overreacting about the McDonald's playdate. I decided to drop the subject.

It was a week before the Christmas events and my assistant called me upset. She was going on and on, so much so, I had to calm her down so I could make sense of what was being said. She stated, "I think the woman is having an affair with my husband!" In disbelief, I quickly calmed her down and asked her to explain why she was thinking her husband and the woman were having an affair. She said, someone told her they saw the two of them together at the Dairy Queen the other night in the parking lot, talking for at least an hour. She said she confronted her husband and the woman about it and they both said it was nothing; they just so happened to be in the parking lot at the same time and the woman wanted his advice about a matter. My assistant expressed to me regardless if it was an innocent conversation or not it just did not look right for him to be in a parking lot talking to her for an hour. She stated, "You know how small this town is, and people love to talk. I do not want my husband's name mixed up with hers and any foolishness!" My assistant said she was going to let Pastor know and ask him for his advice. She needed help with making this "funny feeling" she was having about this woman go away. My assistant just kept saying, "Something isn't right about that woman! She is always in a man's face. She is either in one of the Deacon's faces or somebody's husband face. If it isn't Deacon So & So, it is Brother What's His Name." She continued, "I know her people and that's how some of them get down." I told my assistant to calm down, because it was probably just an innocent conversation. She agreed, but still said she wanted to talk to the Pastor about the woman and how she is always in a man's face. I could see what I was telling her was going in one ear and out the other. She was determined to talk to the Pastor about the issue(s) she had with the woman.

The next time I saw my assistant she said Pastor met with her and told her to calm down, because she was making a big deal out of nothing. She said she felt bad for blowing things out of proportion and apologized to the woman for overreacting. My assistant went on to say she was still going to keep her eyes on the woman, because although she could not place her finger on it, something still was not right about her. Later, I talked to my husband about the situation and he kind of laughed it off saying that the woman was not thinking about my assistant's husband in the way my assistant was trying to make it seem. He said, "They were in a well-lit place, with other people standing around. Your assistant made a big deal out of nothing." My mind flashed back to when the woman was at the Fall Festival laughing and giggling in someone's husband's face, then the week before when she was in one of the Deacon's face at the Christmas rehearsal, and finally when I saw her a couple of days prior sitting at the piano in the Church, tapping on the keys and having a what looked like an intimate conversation with the musician after service. Both she and the musician, who was also a Minister, were sitting on the same little piano bench together, while he was guiding her hands on the keys. Maybe my assistant was making a big deal out of nothing, but then again, maybe she was not.

Eyes Wide Open...And Legs, Too!

One Wednesday Night Bible Study, I forgot to make copies of the printouts for my youth class. The way the Church was set up, the secretary office was in back of the Church. Since I was running late, I decided to take a shortcut through the choir stand side door, to return to my class after making the copies. When I opened the choir door to enter the sanctuary through the choir stands, I noticed that my husband had already commenced teaching Bible Study in the front of the Church. As I looked towards the pews, the very next thing I noticed was the woman sitting on the front row with her legs wide open! I mean wide open…and yes, she was wearing a skirt! I gave her a look of disgust! As soon as our eyes locked, she quickly closed her legs and gazed over at her Bible that was lying on the pew next to her.

I returned to the Youth Bible Study class to pass out the printouts to the young people. I remember being so disgusted with what I had seen, that I could barely teach the class. As soon as the Youth Bible Study had concluded, I went back over to the Adult Bible Study class. But for the first time, the woman had left early. She was nowhere to be found. As soon as I got into the car, I told my husband about what I had seen upon entering the Church. He was puzzled at first, then said he was too engrossed with teaching to notice.

Outraged I said, "What kind of woman sits on the front row of a Church with her legs wide open? That's nasty!"

My husband responded, "Well maybe she did not realize it."

I countered, "She had to realize it! Since when did she start sitting on the front row? No one sits on that row during Bible Study, because we know how you like to walk around in that area, while teaching and demonstrating. She has been coming to Bible Study long enough to know no one sits on that row."

He proceeded to tell me that once again, I was making a big deal out of nothing, just like my assistant had done. He said he did not notice her at all. Maybe he was right. I kept asking myself was I tripping. Maybe my radar was up on her because of the things my assistant had said. The one thing I knew for sure is that I saw what I saw - her sitting on the front pew with her legs wide open, while wearing a skirt. What I saw was not right! I do not care what my husband had to say about the matter. It was at that moment I was convinced what my assistant had said about the woman was true. Something was not right with the woman, and no one could tell me otherwise - including my husband! The next couple of times I saw her, she tried her best to avoid me as much as possible.

Rumors

As time went on, trouble started to brew in the Church between my husband and the Board members. It all started when it was time to build the new Church. People were fighting and disagreeing on the size, style, paint color, pew color, carpet color...everything! I knew from previous experiences with our first Church and from growing up watching and listening to my grandfather talk, that the devil tries to come in every time you are in the foundational stages of building or planning a project. My grandfather always said, "Anytime you are getting ready to build something for the Lord, expect the devil to rear his ugly head."

The devil loves to come in during the laying of the foundation. He wants to stop you before you get started, through division, chaos and confusion. Never underestimate the devil; his job is to steal, kill, and destroy and he comes to do just that - steal, kill, and destroy! The devil will even try to use the people closest to you, to help with his mission. Whenever you attempt to accomplish a major work for the Kingdom of God, problems, pressures and perils come out of nowhere. It is during these battles you discover your strengths and weaknesses. These battles are designed by the devil to break you down mentally. If you allow the devil to control your mind, he can control your body to do anything he wants it do. If you survive these battles, you will find your destiny and purpose for that season in your life. Little did I know I was about to experience the frontline of my own battle...first hand!

I can remember the day like it happened yesterday. I was home, sitting on the sofa when I received a call from one of the Church members saying, "1st Lady there are rumors going around that there are pictures of your husband's car parked at the woman's house." I remember a fire came over me like I never felt before! I said, "What do you mean?" The member responded, "Pastor was at the woman's house the other day and someone took pictures of his car parked in the driveway. The pictures are floating around town. Everyone is talking about the pictures and saying it doesn't look right. I just thought you should know." I thanked the Church member for informing me. Soon after, I called my husband who was at the Church and told him to come home...NOW!

As my husband entered the door, I confronted him about the rumors. I asked him was he at the woman's house, to which he replied, "Yes, I was." My husband said the woman had hysterically called the Church stating one of her children had gotten in trouble at school and she wanted to know if he could come by and pray over the child and her family. He said that he prayed for the family, then left their residence. In his words, "Whoever took the picture was just trying to start some mess. You know how people like to talk in this small town." Since I was not convinced, we decided to call the woman together. Sure enough, her story lined up with my husband's story - Pastor had come over to the house and prayed for her family; the children were even present. After getting off of the phone with the woman, I was so upset with my husband because the people were right, it did not "look right." No wife wants rumors of her husband being at another's woman's house to be floating around town like this – and especially not with pictures of his car in the driveway! I did not know what to think or believe. I knew I trusted my husband. If he said it was not anything, then it was not anything. It was definitely piss-poor judgment on his part, for not taking anyone else from the Church with him when he visited the women and her family. My husband often went to pray for members alone, but this was the first time anyone thought to take a picture of it. Now, the entire town was talking about the news. I had to go to Church with people whispering and talking about my husband in a negative way. Although, I knew the truth, once the rumor got started there was no stopping it!

I was so confused, I knew my husband and some of the Church members were not getting along because of disagreements on the building of the new Church, but why would someone stoop so low as to start rumors about my husband's integrity? It was hurtful, shameful and embarrassing. Yet, I had to hold my head up high, put on my multi-mask and act like it was not affecting me. How could it not affect me, though? This was the same woman I caught with her legs wide open, on the front pew of the Church. Something was not right, and my Spirit was troubled.

I Am From The "A"

After a couple of weeks of dealing with the picture rumors, I continued with my Church duties as if nothing happened. Once the Church members saw I was unbothered, they stopped talking about the situation…at least that is what I thought. Unbeknownst to me, there was a bigger, juicier rumor being spread around town! The woman was now circulating that she was pregnant! Since pictures of my husband's car parked in her driveway were still floating around town, some people began to say she was pregnant by husband. Others said the woman was pregnant by her estranged husband. Still others said it was someone else's baby. To say the least – the woman's pregnancy created a big mess and everyone was talking about it. How in the hell did my husband's name get caught up in this garbage? I remember being so mad and upset that his name was even mentioned in the same sentence as the woman's name. I now knew how my assistant felt when her husband's name was mentioned in the same sentence as the woman. My husband's bad judgement of going into the women's house alone had opened the doors to more rumors, chaos and confusion.

Once again, I had to continue to do my Church duties and act as if it the rumors were not affecting me or our family. I recognized Satan and what he was trying to do, and I was not going to allow him to do succeed. The rumors started affecting my husband, as well as the Church. It was a stressful period in our home and in the Church. It seemed like everything around us was falling apart. Here I was the 1st Lady of the Church and people were saying my husband, the Pastor, got one of the Church members pregnant. To make matters worse, the woman was still a Church member and actively coming to Church every time the doors of the Church were open. It was indeed chaos and confusion. Some people were showing up to Church just to see what was going on between me and her - was I going to speak to her, was she going to speak to me, etc. I felt like I was in a never ending soap opera. It was crazy!

People close to me kept relaying to me the stories the woman was telling other people. The woman was telling some people the rumors were true - she was pregnant with the Pastor's baby. But she was also telling other people it was not true – it was indeed someone else's baby. The entire situation had become a game to her. She was truly basking in the attention the rumors had given her. During that period, the woman would never say a word to me during or after Church service. But she would constantly roll her eyes when she saw me, and make a point to be at every event my husband and I attended, just to keep the gossip going. She would often make sure I would see her rubbing her stomach, while she grinned and smirked. She was taunting me, wanting me to say something to her. This had become a sick game that I did not sign up to play. For months, people were taking their focus off God and focusing on the situation…including me!

Each week, there would be new rumors - she said, he said, they said, etc. The rumors went on to say my husband was going to leave me for the woman and she was going to become the new 1st Lady of the Church. Now that was laughable! No one believed that nonsense. The entire situation had gotten out of hand. I knew I had to do something when the children in my youth groups started to ask me questions about the situation. No married woman wants to answer infidelity questions about her husband; especially if he is a Pastor. I assured the youth not to believe everything they hear. Out of obligation, I continued on with my Church duties. I felt I had to show the Church members that I was spiritually strong; but the human side of me was hurting. It seemed like everything my husband and I had been working hard to build together for our family and future was beginning to be destroyed by this huge lie. Eventually, the woman stopped mentioning other men as being the father and only mentioned my husband's name. What type of sick, twisted, evil game was she playing? I had enough!

One day after Bible Study the woman was in her car waiting on one of her children to come out of the Fellowship Hall, where we were serving food. Rage consumed me, seeing her seated in her car with a smirk on her face. I remember telling one of my close friends, "I will be right back." My friend said, "Where are you going?" I rapidly walked across the Church parking lot, opened the woman's car door and got in the passenger seat of her car. Shocked...I scared her to near death! The woman looked as if she had seen a ghost! She was on the phone with a man at the time. Two of her children were in the back seat. I politely asked them to go into the Church for a moment and tell the youth advisors I said to give them both something to eat, because I needed to talk to their mother. Once the children left the car, I told the woman to hang up the phone...NOW! She quickly let the man on the phone know she would have to call him back. After she hung up the phone, she did not say a word - and she would not look at me. I turned her radio off, then turned my body toward her body.

I stared at the side of her face and asked her, "What is really going on?" She did not answer. I asked again, "WHAT'S REALLY GOING ON? Why are you going around town saying one thing then saying another?"

She said, "I don't know what you're talking about."

I retorted, "The hell if you do not! Do not play stupid with me, because I am not the one! I have one question for you, is this baby my husband's or not?"

She quipped, "You shouldn't believe everything you hear. And you need to get out of my car."

I told her I was not going anywhere and I did not play games! I firmly stated, "You are going around town saying one thing one day, then another thing the next day; messing with people lives! What type of woman are you to play games like this in the Church?"

She started sucking her teeth and talking quickly, asking, "What type of woman are you to get in my car?"

I answered, "The type that's not from here. I'm from Atlanta, and if you weren't pregnant I would beat your fucking ass right now in this car for trying to be a smart ass! While I was speaking, I wrote the word "ass" across her face with my left index finger - to let her know I was not playing with her. Her face expressed pure fear. At that moment I knew she was not worth my anger. Here I was, a 1st Lady, in the woman's car wanting to beat her ass down! It took everything in me not to slap the lips off her face. I told her, "You are not worth it," then I got out of her car. As I was exiting the car, she rolled her window down and said something smart. I quickly turned around to open the door again, but she quickly locked the door.

As I headed back inside the Church, I could see throngs of Church members standing around watching what had just took place in the parking lot. I was so embarrassed. I had allowed myself to act out of character. Some of the Church members were cheering because I had confronted the woman. A few of them said they did not know the 1st Lady was "bout it" and "gangster." As the woman sat in the parking lot, I decided to go into the church to give her children extra food. They had not done anything wrong, and I wanted to show them that I had nothing against them. One thing I knew for sure, she was not that big of a fool. She would not dare get out of her car to come inside to get her children. So, I made sure they left 45 minutes later - with full stomachs and smiles on their faces. Afterwards, I could not help but feel embarrassed by the events that had taken place; especially since it was on the church grounds.

On the way home, I let my husband have it! I said, "See what you've done! I am tired of all of this shit! This is too much!" He was livid that I had acted in such a manner on Church property. I was livid that he had put himself and our family in a position where we had to battle rumors. The entire situation was truly embarrassing, and I knew my actions had just thrown fire on the flames. Unfortunately, at that point I did not care anymore! I did not give a damn! I remember yelling at my husband, "I told you it was something about that woman that was not right! As you can see, that crazy woman doesn't care anything about you being a Pastor, our family or our Church! What the hell is going on? She is playing with our lives and livelihood! I feel like I'm living in a twilight zone right now! People are coming up to me saying don't believe anything she says, she's always been that way, while others are saying she's telling the truth. I'm not from here; I don't know her or these people. I don't know who or what to believe! The only person I know in this town is you, and if you said nothing happened then I believe nothing happened. All of this is going on because you took your ass to that woman's house and because of a damn picture! I hate this! I didn't sign up for this shit!" I felt like my husband could have protected us from all of this mess. Now it was out of control and there was nothing we could do about it! I was aggravated and pissed off, to say the least. My husband assured me that "this too shall pass," and he would make sure of it.

The Truth Will Make You Free

As the new Church was being constructed, multiple Church Business Meetings were held to discuss, in part, details of the progress of the Church. Normally, only a handful of Church members attended the Church Business Meetings. One particular Church Business Meeting, the entire Church was packed. Although no one broached the subject during the meeting, the Church members were concerned about the rumors that were being spread about their Pastor. You could feel the tension in the air. Toward the end of the meeting, the woman walked in the door, with an attitude on her face and sat in the back of the Church. I was surprised, because I had not seen her attend any of our Church functions since I jumped into her car. She was indeed very pregnant, and looked out of place; as if she did not want to be in attendance.

As the Church Business Meeting was about to conclude, my husband boldly addressed the rumors that were circulating about him. It was so quiet in the Church, that you could hear a pin drop. My husband indicated the gossip was very hurtful and the allegations were false. He stated that the other party involved in the vicious rumors was present at the church that night, and she was also willing to go on record and confirm the rumors were not true. My husband asked the woman to stand. As she stood, all eyes and ears were on her...including mine! My husband asked the woman if any of the rumors about them were true. He asked the woman if the two of them had any type of inappropriate relationship. He asked the woman if the baby she was carrying was his child. The woman soundly replied, "No" to each of the questions. After the series of questions, my husband thanked the woman for coming to Church to address the rumors. Then, the woman got up and left the Church.

I was flooded with a sense of relief! I was overjoyed my husband had tackled the matter head on - openly and publicly! Now, the Church could finally go back to focusing on the work of the Lord. Soon after the Church Business Meeting, the woman switched her membership back to her previous Church. Almost everyone was excited that the woman was no longer a part of our Church. Although our Church membership was still growing exponentially, the rumors had begun tearing our Church apart spiritually and emotionally.

I trusted very few people during that period, because I knew I was under spiritual attack. I knew my family was also under spiritual attack. At the end of the day, it was my husband everyone was talking about; the father of my children. That Church Business Meeting was so necessary! My husband had finally given our Church family some ammunition to defend him. People could finally stop spreading the false rumors. We could all go back to focusing on constructing our new edifice. We could all go back to "Changing Lives through Jesus Christ."

God Is Trying To Tell You Something

I became very ill, not too long after the "Truth" meeting. I was so sick that I was vomiting daily. I assumed the stress of the past few months had finally taken a toll on my body. That was not the case. I found out I was pregnant…again! I remember my husband's sheer excitement when I informed him of the news. Although the rumors had caused a slight strain on our marriage, we had made a concerted effort to focus more on our family. Soon after telling my husband the good news, I called home to inform my family. Part of me also wanted to share with my family all the drama that was transpiring in my life, but I was too embarrassed to broach the subject; plus the matter had been addressed to be false. In my mind, there was nothing to tell and all the nonsense had reached its conclusion.

My husband and I shared our pregnancy announcement with a few people in the Church, and it was not long before the entire town knew about the pregnancy. Shortly after the news of my pregnancy broke, the woman started telling people she had lied when she answered the questions in the Church Business Meeting. At that point, I had enough of her nonsense. I could not endure anymore stress, now that I was pregnant! Although some people were dead set on keeping the rumors flying, my main focus was my husband, our children and unborn child. Neither the woman's unborn child, nor her baby's father issues were my concern.

During the first trimester of my pregnancy, I started to have a series of dreams. A cellphone would appear in my dreams every other night. The dreams were very confusing. Each time I had a "cellphone" dream, I shared it my husband. He did not seem to think much of the dreams, but I knew there was a meaning behind the dreams. As time progressed, the dreams became more frequent. There reached a point where every time I went to sleep I would see the cellphone. Ultimately, I realized the cellphone was not just any cellphone; the cellphone in my dream was identical to my husband's old cellphone. Why was I dreaming about my husband's old cellphone? He stopped using his old cellphone months ago when the battery died. I searched for the cellphone and could not find it. I know it sounds strange, but I felt like Lord was trying to tell me something and the cellphone was somehow connected to it.

As weeks passed by, someone mentioned to me the woman had her child and she was still mentioning my husband as the father. As a matter of fact, she was telling anyone who would listen. I was aggravated with the entire situation and had come to the conclusion that the woman was obsessed with my husband and wanted to be me, for whatever reasons. I knew it was not healthy for a person to carry on in the manner she was carrying on. I remember telling the person to just pray for the woman, because that was what I was doing. I rebuked the devil in the woman, in the name of Jesus, every time I had the chance!

Soon after I received news of the woman delivering her baby, rumors on top of rumors, on top of rumors began circulating again. My husband was "supposedly" no longer parking in the driveway anymore, but in the back of her mobile home so no one can see him. What would my husband look like driving our Jaguar through the mud, behind her mobile home? That was absurd! I was sick and tired of being sick and tired, of all of the mess concerning the woman. I was exhausted from defending my husband, while smiling at Church as if I was Superwoman. In reality, I was not! The drama was impacting me mentally and physically. I was not enjoying my pregnancy the way I was used to enjoying pregnancy. On top of that, the latest rounds of rumors were affecting my marriage. All we seemed to talk about those days were the latest rumor. My husband would tell me what he had heard and I would tell him what I had heard. Some of the rumors were laughable, while others were an assassination of his character. We decided to weather the storm together; although the joy we experienced when we first moved to the town was gone.

I lost my passion for leading Church activities. My husband, on the other hand, was still traveling and preaching nonstop. That period, was the first time in my life I wanted to relinquish all of my Church responsibilities. Normally, I loved working with the youth of the Church; they gave me a purpose. Up until that point, whatever I did for them, I gave my all. But the constant onslaught of rumors and allegations were stealing my joy. I no longer had a drive to give it my all. I began to delegate my Church responsibilities to other people, and I would blame it on my pregnancy. The stress was taking a toll on me and my body. I did not want to lose my baby, so I pushed through that period, fully trusting in the Lord!

Nothing was making sense in my mind, including the cellphone dreams. I had to find my husband's old cellphone. I was not going to get any sleep if I did not find it! I tore the whole house up looking for the cellphone. I finally found it in a basket that had miscellaneous cords and batteries. What now? I tried to charge the cellphone, but it was still broken. I thought maybe I will put my cellphone battery in cellphone and see if it will work. Sure enough, it worked! I waited for the cellphone to turn on, and then I hit the button to see the call log. I remember feeling as if a bolt of lightning had struck my chest! All of a sudden I could not breathe! It felt as if an elephant was standing on my chest. I fell to my knees. I could not believe what I was seeing! I was viewing a plethora of calls between my husband and the woman, dating back an entire year! I felt like I was going to blackout! I depressed the button to display the text messages and I was absolutely stunned! My husband was having an affair with the woman! All of a sudden, the room started spinning! I cried from the depths of my soul! This could not be real! I must be dreaming! Noooo...not my husband! I was wailing and hollering at the top of my lungs! I cried like a person does after they get the news that one of their loved ones has unexpectedly passed away. I was so thankful my children were in their rooms with the door closed, watching cartoons. I could not wrap my mind around what I was reading! It was too much! That entire time, my husband had been lying to me and everyone else! I felt betrayed! How could he do this to me? To us? To our family? To the Church? I remember just sobbing and asking, "Why? Why? Why would he do this, God? Why?" It seemed like my soul had departed; I felt empty.

After what appeared to be an hour of mourning, I called my husband, who was at the Church. I was crying uncontrollably, while cussing him out at the same time! I was yelling and cussing at him! He could barely make sense of what I was saying. I told him that all his shit would be out in the front yard when he came home! After hanging up the phone in his face, all I could see was red! Everything around me turned red! In rage, I ran to our closet - with tears streaming down my face. Yelling and screaming, I started grabbing his clothing, opened our front door and threw it out in the yard. His expensive, tailored suits were landing in the bushes and dirt. His reptile shoes were strewn in the grass and driveway. His designer cuff links were lying in the street. I threw his items as far as I could toss them, and prayed for it to rain! I continued marching from the back of the house to the front of the house, with hands full of his belongings; launching them out the door. I remember saying over and over again, "How could he do this to me?" The more I muttered the words, the madder I became. I started searching for the scissors, because I was determined to cut the crotch and knees out all his pants and the elbows out all of his shirts and suit coats. Normally, I always had tons of scissors, but during that moment I could not find a single pair! I think it was God's way of protecting me from me. As

I was tearing up the house searching for scissors, my husband came through the door with a handful of his clothing that had been thrown in the yard. I hollered at him, "Why? You are a liar! How could you cheat on me?"

I felt like I was going to pass out! I was shaking uncontrollably. I could not believe what was happening! I remember throwing anything I could get my hands on at him, while he was trying to explain himself. I did not want to hear his pathetic pleas about how he was sorry and never meant to hurt me. "Sorry? Sorry! Your ass is sorry alright...a lying, sorry motherfucker!" I had never cursed that much in my life. But at that moment, it was gratifying to call him every name in the curse book! I could see the hurt in his eyes, but I did not care! I wanted him out of my face! Reflecting on that moment, I am extremely happy I never found a pair of scissors. Our children began to come out of their rooms. I did not want them to see me in a hysterical state. I asked my husband to leave and he obliged.

I locked myself in the bathroom and wept. How could he do this to us? I started to think back to the time she first called my home. I took the cellphone out my pocket and sure enough, the texts dated back to before the day she called my home, trying to get her daughter and my daughter to become playmates. Before she was a member of our Church, she was already sleeping with my husband! The ladies at the Fall Festival were correct! The woman was out there to get somebody's husband - mine! I got queasy thinking about the times and dates, while reading the awful text messages! The situation was sick! Sick! It was not too long after I had my third child that the woman and my husband initiated their adulterous relationship!

I repeatedly dialed my husband, just so I could call him every other derogatory name I could think of; names I had not previously called him! I hung up in his face and then called back to cuss him out some more! I did not let him get in a word. I did not want to hear what he had to verbalize. The writing was on the wall; well, it was in the texts. There was nothing my husband could say to remedy the situation! God had alerted me of his infidelity through my dreams.

Then it hit me - the woman's baby! I was so caught up by the fact that my husband was having an affair that I forgot about the woman's baby! Her baby was possibly my husband's baby! I snapped, while on the phone, and began to uncontrollably yell and scream at him; to the point I could not breathe. I felt like an elephant was standing on my chest again! Hearing that I could barely talk or breathe, my husband said he was coming back home. He did not want the children to be worried or see me in my current state. My husband came back home. I cussed him some more and threw more objects at him, for good measure. Then, I went into our bedroom closet. I did not want to see his face! I was disgusted by even looking at him! How could he do this to our family? I remember saying over and over again, "I do not know you! Who are you?" I was crying so much that my contacts fell out my eyes.

I quickly realized I was back in a closet again - in darkness! It was different this time, though. I had made a promise, years ago, I would never get so low that I would yearn to stay in a dark closet again. I immediately opened the door, went into the bathroom, lit a candle and began to pray and cry out to the Lord for guidance. I begged the Lord to help me! He had to help me! I had nowhere else to turn! As I petitioned the Lord, I began to hear a loud horn; it was a train whistle. The train whistle was so loud that it felt like I was standing right next to the train tracks. But, I knew the nearest train tracks were on the other side of town. As I continued to pray and ask God for guidance, the whistle got louder. The third whistle was even louder than the previous two whistles! It was at that moment I realized God was with me. He heard my prayers me and saw my tears! They Holy Spirit enveloped me and I praised God like I had never praised Him before! I knew He was with me; I could feel Him in the bathroom. I started shouting, "Thank you for helping me Lord!

Thank you, Jesus, for helping me! I need you right now! Please help me! I know you are able, Lord!"

I was praising God in advance. Until this day, I have no idea how I was able to praise the Lord, when in reality I should have been angry. Yes I was still hurting. Yes, I was still crying. But for a brief moment in my bathroom, I felt the comfort of the Most High God. As I sat on the bathroom rug, I sobbed until there were no more tears left. When I rose up from the bathroom floor to look at myself in the mirror, and it appeared as if I had been in a fight. My eyes were swollen from all the crying I had done. I did not want my children to see me disheveled and I did not want to look at my husband's face, so I decided to sleep on the bathroom floor for the night. I found comfort in the light from the candle and knowing God was present with me.

What A Friend...

The next day, I could not bear to look at my husband. I was still in a state of shock. How could he do such a thing? I wanted answers and I wanted them immediately! As my husband entered the room, I told him I wanted to know the truth! I wanted to know everything! How had their relationship materialized? When, where, why? He told me their relationship initiated when I took a break from Church; right after having our third child. The woman repeatedly showed up to his preaching engagements. They met through a mutual friend, she was supposedly dating. The woman asked the mutual friend for my husband's phone number, because she had some biblical questions to ask him. Over time, the woman began flirting with him and he eventually reciprocated. My husband then said, "Telling you this information isn't going to help; it's only going to make matters worse! Nothing good can come from divulging the details of the affair." With tears rolling down his face, he expressed his remorse and how much he never meant to hurt me. I did not want to hear it! I wanted the truth!

"So, you mean to tell me you have been sleeping with the woman all this time?"

He replied, "I am sorry!"

"You had this woman in our Church?"

He responded, "I told her not to join the Church, but she joined anyway."

I angrily ranted, "This is sick! Sick! I do not know you anymore! Who are you?"

My husband repeatedly apologized and begged for forgiveness. "I did not mean for this to happen! The situation got out of control! Once it got out of control with the rumors, I did not know how to respond. I never meant to hurt you!"

I retorted, "You never meant to hurt me? No, you never meant to get caught! You have hurt me beyond repair! How could you? You had a baby! A BABY!"

He quickly said, "Nooooooo…I do not know if that baby is mine."

I screamed, "What do you mean you do not know?"

He answered, "I do not know! She says the baby is mine, but I used protection!"

I countered, "Do you hear yourself! I cannot believe this mess! This is too much! How could you? This is sick! You both stood in Church and lied! How could you?

Looking defeated, he said, "I know! The situation got out of hand and I tried to do damage control. I knew if I told the truth, I was going to lose my family and possibly the Church. I did not want to lose you! You and our children are all I have in life! I am sorry! Please forgive me!"

I responded adamantly, "No!" "What am I supposed to do now? Forgive you? You ruined us! You ruined our family! A baby? I am pregnant with your child right now! What am I supposed to do?"

I received a reality check when I realized, for a couple of months, the woman and I were both pregnant at the same time. The thought made me so ill that I told my husband to leave me alone! He agreed and went into the other room. I lied in the bed with all types of thoughts going through my head. What is going to happen to my family? What is going to happen to the Church? At that time no one from the Church knew I knew the truth. How could I go back to Church and face the Church members knowing what I knew? How could I return to directing the Youth Department? I had assured them the allegations against the Pastor were false! Now I was a liar, too! How could I face my family - my father and mother? How could I explain this deranged situation to them? What was I going to do? My head felt as if it was going to explode.

I wanted more answers! I ran into the room with my husband and asked if he had seen the woman's baby.

"Yes, I saw him in the grocery store. We agreed to meet up in the same aisle. I assure you, he doesn't look like me! I don't think he is my baby."

I do not know what prompted me to ask the next question, but I asked, "What did the woman name the child?"

My husband looked at me and then looked down. When my husband announced the baby's name, it was like a knife cut through my heart. The baby's name was the same name my husband had wanted to give our son. At the time, I had objected to the name because a little boy in our Church already carried the name.

I exploded! "How could you? How could you give the baby THAT name?"

He said, "Noooooo! I did not name him; she did! I had nothing to do with the baby's name! All her children have the same first letter in their names. She wanted him to have a biblical name that had the same letter. I had nothing to do with naming the baby! I promise you!"

I was beyond hurt and had heard enough! This was insane! I could not believe it! The room started to spin again. I had to get out of the house! I left the house. I jumped in the car and drove to the Church as fast as I could. I had to be driving over 90 miles per hour! Thankfully, no one was at the Church when I arrived. It was nighttime and the only lights that was visible in the Church were the lights from the exit sign and the outside street lights that were shining through the stained glass windows. After headed into the sanctuary, I ran to the altar! I fell on my knees and started praying until my mouth was literally dry. I asked God for help and strength. I was emotionally drained and weak. I had not eaten anything since reading the text messages. I stayed at the altar, on my knees, for hours. A Spirit of comfort came over me, so much so that I fell asleep at the altar. When I awoke, it was 3am. I decided to drive back home to get some rest. On my drive home, I do not know what happened, but I had the sudden urge to tell someone. Who do I tell? Who can I trust?

I arose extremely early the next day and decided to go back to the Church, before anyone arrived. On the way to Church, I decided to call one of the Church members I had become close with over the past few months. She had been a blessing to me, by helping out with the care of my children; while I fulfilled my Church duties. I trusted her with my children and I rarely trusted anyone with my children. She was the type of person who would give you the shirt off her back. She was always concerned about my wellbeing and continuously called to see how I was doing when a bad rumor would come out about my husband. I had grown to appreciate her friendship. On that day, I decided to ask her to meet me at the Church. She agreed, but I could hear the worry in her voice when she asked if I was feeling well. No, I was not feeling well, and I knew I had to share my thoughts with someone else.

When my friend arrived at the Church, she could tell I was visible upset and had been crying. I decided to tell her everything I knew, from the cellphone dreams, to our Pastor admitting to having an affair with the woman. She experienced the same emotional fit I had experienced, when I told her everything. She was hurt, upset and shocked. She said, "But they both stood up in Church and said the rumors were not true! I was there! I heard them both say the rumors were not true!" Just like me, she could not believe what I was telling her. My friend had so many questions that I did not have the answers to yet. At that moment, it was therapeutic for me to get everything I was thinking off my chest. It was comforting knowing I had someone I could talk to about my horrible situation. Of course, my friend promised not to say a word. I was happy I could trust her.

My husband did not know if he was the father of the woman's baby or not. I could not allow myself to worry about that matter too much. The last thing I wanted to experience was the pain of another miscarriage. I decided to take things one day at a time. Some days I cried all day long. Other days, I was so angry I felt like I was going to do something I would later regret. For two weeks, I went into a deep depression. I literary stayed in the bed for two weeks. Every time I thought about my husband's selfish actions, I would breakdown and cry to the point of having panic attacks. That was my first encounter with panic attacks. Panic attacks were very scary and the only thing that would stop them was when my husband would come into the room and start praying over me and quoting Bible verses. For some reason, that always calmed me down. It was so ironic that the person who hurt me and triggered the panic attacks was the person helping me control them.

I was on an emotional roller coaster. Some days were better than other days. The better days were when I had long conversations with my friend. She knew how to listen. Sometimes, that was all I needed. Other days, God would speak to me through a popular Bishop, who had a show on the Christian network. It seemed like when I was at my lowest points, I would turn on the television and the Bishop would be preaching a sermon that was tailor made for my situation! Until this day, I believe God was using the Bishop to help heal me.

Every day, I felt like I was regaining my strength through prayer, reading my Bible, talking to my friend and listening to the Bishop's sermons. I knew I had to get myself together for the child I was carrying and for my children. My children knew something was wrong, because I was not my usual jovial self when I played with them. Our family had been torn apart and I was determined to put the pieces back together, even though I knew it would never be the same. My close friend did an outstanding job of calling and checking on me. She made sure I was eating and taking care of myself. At that time, I needed her more than she would ever know. She was a God send! I was very thankful I could trust her, and her sincere heart.

Church members started to question my whereabouts, including the youth. I knew I had responsibilities. I decided to return to Church, even though I was still upset with my husband. It was so hard to face the Church members. Although I had knowledge of my husband's affair, I did not want to be the one to tell them. At that moment, I was only focused on my pregnancy; I knew I could not handle any more stress.

My husband preached as powerfully and passionately as ever. People were still joining the Church in droves. But I tuned out all his sermons. His words went into one ear and came out the other. I closed my eyes for most of the service, and it felt good. I was in Church, but my mind was somewhere else. After service people could tell something was wrong, but they just assumed I was enduring a rough pregnancy.

The next week, a Pastor, who was one of my grandfather's dearest friends, was scheduled to preach a 3 night revival at our Church. The year before, my husband had extended the invitation for this Pastor to conduct our revival. He was also a close friend of my husband. The Pastor happily accepted. Talk about perfect timing! I decided to go to Church each night, and each night I was blessed by the sermon the Pastor preached! It felt good to see a friendly face from back home. Each night, the Pastor's sermons touched my soul, to the point it felt like I was going to pass out! My eyes were swollen shut each night, from the tears I cried. The sermon the Pastor preached on the final night of Revival was especially overwhelming. I did not want the Pastor to leave. When it was time for the altar prayer, the Pastor walked down, out of the pulpit, and prayed for me. I fell to my knees and started weeping like I had never wept before in Church. The ushers had to carry me into a room. Some of the Church members knew something was wrong, because I had never carried on in such a manner.

I remember at least 5 or 6 Church members coming into the room and circling around me. They started to pray for me. The Spirit was so high in the room that some of the ones that were praying begin to shout and cry, too. After the prayer I felt a little lighter. God had sent people to come help carry my burdens. After service, I was waiting for my husband to finish talking to some of the Church members so we could go home.

One of the mothers of the Church, who was in the prayer circle, told me, "Tomorrow, I am going to take you to lunch. It will be me, and two other Church members who are older and wise women."

I said, "No, thank you. I won't be feeling up to it."

She responded, "You do not have a choice, my dear. You need a break. Let us treat you out for a day. Saying 'no' is not an option." She was not backing down and I knew I had to attend. No biggie, I was just going to put on my multi-mask and do my best job of pretending everything was well.

I went out to lunch with the older women, and I thought I was doing a great job pretending I was well. But these 3 wise women could see right through my mask. They knew I was experiencing a deep hurt, and they were not going to let me go until they had helped me. After lunch, the wise women told me they had rented out the conference room at the library in the next town. They said, "It will just be the four of us. We are not here to judge you. God sent us to help you." The wise women let me know that I could get anything off my chest without the fear of it leaving that room. I immediately wondered: What should I do? Should I trust these women? At that point, I did not really know who to trust. I knew my soul was tired and I did not have any family present. Only one person that I was close to me knew the truth. I prayed a quick prayer. God assured me I could trust the wise women. As I told them everything, they were in state of shock and disbelief. Of course they had heard the rumors about my husband – our Pastor. But they did not believe the rumors were true.

The wise women all began to shed sorrowful tears, as I sat lifeless in the chair. They surrounded me - one reading Scriptures, one "laying hands" with oil and one praying. The wise women rebuked the devil that was rising up and every wicked plan the enemy had assigned against me. The wise women also began to "speak life" into me. They said, "I shall live, and not die!" The wise women reminded me about my beautiful children and the baby I was carrying. Not only did they speak life into me, they spoke life into my family. The wise women prayed for my husband and children. God used those three women in a mighty way! He sent them to show me I was not alone, and He had heard my prayers and saw my tears. The wise women prayed until I began to praise and thank God. One of the wise women said, "She's back! Thank you, Jesus! She's going to be alright. Don't let the devil run you! You run him back to hell! God is going to get the glory out of this situation! Watch and see! You don't have to worry about us telling a soul. We are here for you and your children. We want to see you healthy and prospering. Call any one of us, anytime and we will be there for you!" I cannot express in words how I felt after the three wise women dropped me back off at home. I had a renewed mind and spirit. The wise women reminded me of what a merciful God I serve. They reminded me that God would never leave me nor forsake me. The enemy was out to destroy me and my family, but I was not going to allow it to happen!

Women To Women

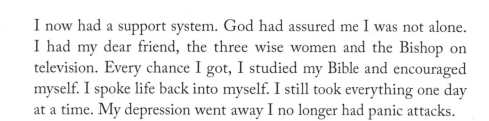

I now had a support system. God had assured me I was not alone. I had my dear friend, the three wise women and the Bishop on television. Every chance I got, I studied my Bible and encouraged myself. I spoke life back into myself. I still took everything one day at a time. My depression went away I no longer had panic attacks.

One day while reading my Bible, the phone rang. I checked the caller idea and it was the woman's number. What? I could not answer that phone quickly enough! My husband was at Church at the time. I said, "Hello." When she began to talk, her voice sounded like cat claws screeching across a chalkboard in my ear.

"Your husband loves you so much…but did he tell you I had his baby."

By the tone of her voice I could tell she was angry and attempting to rile me up, too. I decided not to give the devil in her what he wanted.

I countered, in a calm voice, "He said he doesn't think that it's his child."

"It's his child."

"Did you get a DNA test?"

"No, but I know this is his child."

"Sorry, but I don't believe anything you say. You have some nerves calling my house, though."

"I just want to tell you your husband has been lying to both of us."

"Oh, really? Both of you are liars. You both stood up in Church and lied."

She got defensive and snapped, "I only stood in church and lied because he told me to do it."

I laughed aloud and said, "You're a grown woman. You lied because you wanted to lie! Do not put all the blame on him. Both of you will have to answer to God."

She attempted to blame some more stuff on my husband, but I was unfazed. I kept throwing in the woman's face that he was married and a Pastor when she met him. She could stop attempting to play the victim role. It was not as if she was an innocent woman who unknowingly started to sleep with a married man. God had to have been with me, because prior to my meeting with the wise women I would have cursed her out - from the top of her head to the soles of her feet...2 times, maybe even 3! By that time, I had become a professional at cursing someone out; due to all the recent practice I had my husband. My timing and delivery was impeccable.

In an effort to get under my skin, the woman told me some intimate details of her affair with my husband. Once she figured out she could not upset me, she then started to talk about God and quote verses from the Bible. I told the woman she could not quote Scriptures to me. I knew the Bible well...and I knew that both her and my husband would reap what they had sown! I told her thank you for calling me. Then, we both hung up our phones.

As soon as the conversation ended with the woman, I called my husband at the Church. I told him to come home...NOW! While he headed home, I got dressed and got our children dressed. Next, I called the woman back. I let her know that my husband and I were on our way to her home, because I wanted to talk to both of them together! The woman was shocked, but agreed. She stated one of her children was home. I asked if there was a place in her home for all of us to speak privately. She said, "Yes, the children can play out in the yard, while we talk." I agreed. It was a good thing the children were coming, because I knew having them with me would prevent me from beating the woman's ass.

When my husband arrived home, I told him to take me to the woman's house...NOW! Although he tried to talk me out of the decision, he knew I was not playing. As we pulled up to the woman's mobile home, I was surprised to see that it looked condemned. I keenly watched how my husband expertly bypassed the makeshift driveway. He parked behind the mobile home - invisible from the street view - just like the rumors had stated. It took everything in me not to slap him at that moment. I knew I had to stay prayed up, because I was about to enter into the home of a woman who was having an affair with my husband.

The woman opened her back door and greeted my family, along with her daughter. Her daughter, not knowing the nature of our visit, was genuinely excited to see us. After all, my husband had baptized her, along with her brothers. As we walked into the sitting area, I took a good look at the woman for the first time - from head to toe. I did not have one jealous bone in my body when I looked at the woman. Physically speaking, I had absolutely no reason to be jealous of her.

When the children went outside to play, we all sat down. The baby was on the love seat, asleep in his car seat. It was quiet in the room, as I looked at the baby sleeping peacefully. I did not think the baby looked like my husband, nor any of our children. The baby looked like the woman's other children, she had conceived with her estranged husband. I informed the woman I was not convinced the baby was my husband's child.

The woman said, "It's his child."

I responded, "I do not believe anything either one of you says. You both are liars."

Again, the woman tried to explain her part in the lie. The entire time my husband was sitting in disbelief that he was even in this "meeting." I continuously reminded the woman they both were going to reap what they had sown. I knew I had struck a nerve each time I made the statement, because the woman would get extremely quiet. Therefore, I said it every chance I got.

Once my husband snapped out of his catatonic state, he apologized to both me and the woman. First, he turned to me and apologized for breaking his marital vows and publicly embarrassing me, our family and Church. Then, he turned to the woman and apologized for leading her on in any kind of way.

With the next breath, he firmly told the woman, "But, you know I have always made it crystal clear I would never leave my wife for you."

"Yes, you have made that clear. But you have also told me you love me."

"Yes, but I love my wife and children more. I apologize to both of you."

The baby woke up and I immediately jumped up to take him out of his car seat. I do not know what came over me, but I felt a certain urge to want to hold him. As I held him, so many emotions came over me. I could not believe I was holding the baby of the woman who had an affair with my husband. Until this day, I still cannot believe it! As my husband continued speaking, the woman watched me like a hawk as I held her child. Holding the baby made me realize the baby and I were both victims of the sick and twisted game my husband and the woman were playing. Being pregnant myself, I felt sorry for the baby. I told the woman, "Since I don't believe anything you say, we need to get a blood test." My husband agreed and said if, in fact, the baby was his child, he would take care of him. We all decided to keep our meeting a secret until a blood test had been completed.

I left the woman's house feeling empowered for the moment. My main concerns were my children and unborn child. At that point, I recognized the devil was after my mind. I knew I had to be strong - for my children's sake and for the people in the Church. I had to mentally prepare myself for when the news broke about my husband's lie.

Approximately three hours after leaving the woman's house, I started receiving phone calls saying the woman was going around town telling people I had been at her house with my husband, holding her baby. She even divulged all the details of the conversation the three of us had at her home. The people who relayed the story to me talked about how crazy the woman sounded. They knew I would never go over the woman house and hold her baby. Although I knew the story was true, I never corrected them. I just laughed it off and prayed for the woman. I chose not to entertain the woman's games, because I did not want to lose my unborn child. I had finally confirmed the woman was the main person leaking information, in hopes the information would get back to me. All I had was my family and Church. I recognized the devil was out to destroy them both. I refused to let that happen!

Mirror, Mirror On The Wall...

As more rumors spread, I continued going to Church with my head held high. I was determined not to let the devil win. The Church members were excited because the construction of the new Church was finally completed. We had made history as a Church family, because we kept moving forward in spite of all the headaches and heartbreaks, ups and downs and trial and tribulations. Now, we were all about to walk through the doors of our new edifice. The talk of the town had transitioned from the woman and her baby to our state of the art new Church building. The transition felt like a great victory.

For months, we were experiencing amazing worship services in the new Church. We were fulfilling our mission of "Changing Lives through Jesus Christ." People were joining our Church so rapidly that even our new Church was full on Sunday mornings. During that time, my husband and I focused on ensuring I had a healthy baby. We even put our marital issues aside for our children's sake. Our children needed a sense of normalcy in our household. As a couple, we took things one day at a time. Each day, my husband expressed deep remorse for his actions. Frankly, I did not know what to do. I loved my husband, but he had caused me so much hurt and pain.

One day, I was home alone and heard a knock on the door. The Sheriff was at my door to serve papers to my husband, to submit his DNA for child support. Reality hit me. This could possibly be my husband's child. Having an affair and lying to cover it up was terrible as it was, but fathering a child with another woman, while being married was one of the worst things a husband can do to his wife. On top of all of all that, my husband was a Pastor!

I tried to mentally prepare myself for the gossip that was certain to spread once my husband was summoned to the small, public courthouse to submit DNA samples. Part of me knew that once he entered those doors there was no turning back. Surely, the town was going talk again…and they had every right to talk. How was I going to face the latest round of drama? I was in the last trimester of my pregnancy. I was doing well; in spite of my circumstances.

Everything changed, weeks later, when I received another knock at the door from the same Sheriff. He delivered the DNA results. I quickly opened the results, and to my dismay it stated my husband was the father of the woman's baby! My heart was ripped out of my body! I called my husband to tell him the news, and he immediately hurried home. All I could do was stare at the results, and the pictures that accompanied the results. The DNA results had a picture of my husband atop, the baby in the middle and the woman on the bottom. The pictures made me so sick, I started to vomit. When my husband walked through the door, I yelled and screamed, "How could you do this to us? Why? What have you done?" He started to cry and said over and over again how sorry he was about the entire chain of events. I did not want to hear anything my husband had to say. I felt numb. For the next three days, I cried until I had no more tears. I could not eat nor sleep. I had checked out mentally.

To add insult to injury, the woman had made hundreds of copies of the DNA papers and passed them out at local beauty salons, barber shops, buffet places, grocery stores…you name it! The woman pranced around town as if she had won a trophy. She went to churches that we were affiliated with us, stood up during the visitors' recognition, then said her name and introduced the baby as my husband's child. I had never witnessed so much chaos and confusion. Our phone rang off the hook. Other Pastors and 1st Ladies repeatedly called to inform us of the woman's antics. I stopped answering the phone.

I fell back into a deep depression. The situation was tragic; it was too much for my brain to process. My mind went into overdrive trying to analyze how much damage my husband's actions were going to cause our marriage, children and Church! The chain of events was so traumatic that it caused me to experience short term memory loss. All of a sudden, I could not remember anything I had done, within five minutes of doing it. I would literally stand in a spot for an hour attempting to remember what I had done moments before. I could not even remember activities I had performed with my children. My mind was blank. It was so frustrating! My world was falling apart. I was lost and confused. I was empty and distraught. Until this day, I cannot remember the birth of my middle child or even her as a baby. I get sad when I think about that fact. I hope one day those memories come back to me, like some other memories came back to me years later.

One day I was in my bathroom just staring in the mirror. I did not recognize myself. I was in pain and I wanted to rid myself of my depressed feeling. Without thinking twice, I grabbed the pair of scissors out of the drawer and started cutting off all of my hair from the root...yes, the root! After I was finished, I stared at myself in the mirror for an hour. I finally looked how I felt like on the inside - empty.

During my next doctor's visit, my doctor noticed the dramatic change in my appearance. She was deeply concerned for me and the baby. After running tests, the doctor noticed my levels were off and I was losing weight. She immediately put me on bedrest and demanded I tell her what was going on to cause the changes. I told the doctor everything and she sat down on the examine table next to me and started to cry. She shared with me that she had gone through a similar situation a couple of years ago. As she was crying and hugging me, I sat immobile, just staring at the wall. I had no more emotions. No more tears. No more energy. No more strength to even hug her back. The doctor said I needed to have an emergency C-section. The baby was stressed and so was I. She scheduled the procedure for the following week.

Although I was disappointed my baby had to come early, I had done all I could do to make it to that point in my pregnancy. I was tired. Furthermore, I knew once people found out my husband was indeed the father of the woman's baby, they were going to be heartbroken. I could no longer protect the hearts of the people from feeling pain and disappointment. I realized I had placed myself in the middle of God's will. It was not my responsibility to try to control the outcome. My responsibility was to fully trust God.

I was overjoyed that my mother came in town the week of my C-section! She had no idea how much her visit meant to me. Her timing could not have been better! My mother's presence was a stabilizing force; even though she was unaware of the devastating chain of events that had recently occurred in my life. At that moment, I was a child who needed her mother. For those few days, my mother was everything that I needed her to be...plus more!

My husband and I joyfully welcomed our fourth child - our third beautiful baby girl - into the world! She was adorable! Three weeks later, my husband informed me, after praying over the matter, he had decided to resign from his position as Senior Pastor of the Church. He said he had brought shame and dishonor on God and the Church, and he realized the hurt, pain and damage his actions had caused. The following Sunday, my husband announced his resignation during Sunday Service. He did not explain the reason why he was stepping down; some people knew, while others did not. He just stated God was taking him in another direction, and he offered the Church encouraging words of hope and peace. At that time, my husband thought openly admitting he had fathered a child with the woman would cause more harm and shame to the Church.

Unfortunately, I did not get a chance to return to the Church to say my "goodbyes," because I had just given birth. That period should have been one of the happiest times in our lives. We were living the American dream; we had a beautiful family, we were making a positive impact in people's lives and we were highly successful in our fields. My husband's selfishness and pride turned our American dream into a horror story. Now, another woman was in the streets telling everyone who would listen that my husband was the father of her baby. The entire situation was horrible!

Starting Over

Shortly after resigning, the Lord led my husband to organize a new Church. My husband was excited for an opportunity to prove he was still a great Pastor - he had just made a series of bad decisions. My husband had always preached sermons about second chances, and now he wanted a second chance. We exhausted our savings account, in order to finance the start of our new Church. Admittedly, the birth of our daughter had brought us closer; although I was still hurt by my husband's actions.

We received and overwhelming amount of love and support. The community rallied around my husband's vision of a new Church. After all, he was still a highly sought-after Pastor. The first Church service was held at the local high school. The atmosphere was electric! The worship and preaching was anointed! To our amazement, 121 people joined the Church at the first service! People came up to me and said that everyone makes mistakes. They wanted to support me and my family.

As things took off with the new Church, I started receiving emails from the woman on Myspace. She sent emails questioning how much my husband loved me and misquoted Scriptures to justify her affair with my husband. The woman was clearly trying to get a response from me, but I knew I was smarter than her. I was not going to leave a paper trail of me cursing her out, for her to pass around town like she did the DNA papers. The woman sent multiple emails stating her child was better than my children and looked better than my children, etc. She was taunting me. As badly as I wanted to tell the woman where to go and how to get there, I never once responded. That was so hard for me. Since I did not give the woman the reaction she wanted, she started calling our house - all hours of the day and night - playing on the phone. On one occasion, she called and said her cousins were on their way to my house to beat me up. By that time, I was fed up. I told her I would be on the porch waiting on them. I sat in a chair on my front porch until the street lights lit up. Needless to say, no one ever showed up.

I reminded my husband of the mess he had created, each time I had to deal with the woman's childish antics! Things got worse when the woman started following me around town. If I was in a store, all of a sudden she would show up in the store. The town was small, but it was not that small. Her pop-ups happened on several occasions. She would never say a word to me; just stare and act like she was shopping. One time, I looked in my rearview mirror and noticed the woman was three cars behind me at the McDonald's drive thru. I left McDonald's, without ordering, and drove across the street to another restaurant just to see if she would follow me. Sure enough, she followed me to the other restaurant!

I did not sign up to play her demented games. I could not understand why she was after me! She was the one who had slept with my husband, delivered his child and made sure the entire world knew she had a child from a married Pastor – not me. She had already helped to cause chaos and confusion in our Church, which was our livelihood. What more did the woman want?

The straw that broke the camel's back occurred when I took my baby for her three month checkup. After the checkup, one of the nurses, who I recognized from a Church we once visited, came into the room and said, "We do not want any trouble in our office today. We are going to escort you out the back door." I said, "For what?

The nurse replied, "Well, the woman is here for her appointment today, too, and we do not know what she is capable of doing." I had never been treated as such in my life! I had never been escorted out of anyone's back door! That was too much! Too much!

Soon after this incident, the woman started to inbox me messages on Facebook, saying how much she and her child love spending my money from child support. It became clear, the woman was obsessed with me and she was not going to stop messing with me. I had to stop her!

I made copies of all the emails the woman had sent to me on Myspace and Facebook, as well as the phone logs of her calling my home. Then, I filed a restraining order against the woman. The woman came to the hearing alone. I came to the hearing with five witnesses, including my father - who now knew the entire story after one day being at my home when the woman continued to call and play on the phone. I did not want my husband to be in the courtroom that day, because I did not want to make the hearing about him. It was time to settle the score with the woman who was following and threatening me, sending derogatory emails and saying awful things about me and my beautiful children. I had enough!

The woman came into the court room very cocky, as if she was going to prove to the judge that she had the right to stalk me just because she had a child from my husband. The judge asked the woman if she was being vindictive. She proudly responded, "Yes, a little." The judge asked her a series of other questions. After the woman's responses, the judge firmly told the woman that she disgusted him! The judge did not even need to ask any of my witnesses to speak, he had heard enough. The judge told me that if the woman ever came within 200 yards of me or my family...lock her up! The judge turned to the woman and said, "If this lady is in the store, you leave! If this lady is walking down the street, you go the opposite direction!" Next, he turned to me and said, "If she tries to contact you in any way again, call the police and lock her up!" Angrily, the judge told the bailiff to immediately get the woman out of his court room!

As the bailiff escorted the woman out the court room, she cried and told me and my witnesses that we were all going to hell. We all laughed so hard that tears were coming out our eyes! I felt victorious! I had pleaded my case to the judge and I had won! I was surrounded by people who loved and cared for me, including my dear friend and father. I was not alone in my fight against the enemy. That courtroom victory was symbolic to me, because God showed me that no weapon formed against me would prosper. In the end, God was the ultimate judge and He would not allow the enemy to go unchecked for too long.

Roughly a month after getting the restraining order, the woman sent another email; this time to our family shared email account. I contacted the police. The policeman read the email and confirmed that it violated the restraining order. He told me I could press charges to have the woman placed in jail. He went on to say she had committed a felony. Then, he asked if I wanted to press charges on the woman. When the policeman said "felony," for a quick second all I could think about were the woman's children being without their mother for at least a year. Waiting for my answer, I told the policeman not to worry about it.

I had every right to send the woman to jail, after the months of torment and torture she had put me through, but I chose to take the high road - for the sake of her children. That moment made me feel empowered! I had the opportunity to wreak havoc on the woman's life. I could have easily turned her life upside down, just like she had tried to do to my life. But, I chose to let God fight my battle.

In my mind, the woman had already been defeated. After all, she was a pitiful woman. She was a woman who had gotten impregnated by a married Pastor. She lied about the relationship in Church. She stalked the Pastor's wife. She had a restraining order filed against her. And she put herself in a position to be incarcerated. How pitiful! I started to pray for woman, because she definitely needed prayers.

Flipping the script, I sent word by the "street committee" to inform the woman the next time she even thought about sending an email to me or following me, I would have her locked up and not think twice about the decision! That was not a rumor. That was a fact! I assume the message reached the woman, because I have not been bothered or contacted by the woman ever again! God is good!

No Test, No Testimony!

My dreams returned, but they were different. In my dreams, I would be on stage speaking to crowds of thousands of people. The crowds would begin applauding and then I would awaken. I shared my dreams with my husband. I asked him to help me decipher the meaning of my dreams. My husband said, "Ask the Lord for clarity, He will reveal the meaning of your dreams."

One night, God awoke me from my dream. Although I was awake, I felt like I was still dreaming. God physically led me outside to look at the stars. While outside, He revealed details about my future. He explained to me that I would one day help His people. He told me I had to endure the trials I went through, because He was using my life as an example for others. God said every tear I shed had a divine purpose. He elaborated by letting me know my testimony was filled with virtue and value, and it would resonate in the hearts of the masses. He informed me I had a mission to minister, teach and preach His Word to the least, last and lost. And my ministry would heal broken hearts, renew minds, restore souls and resurrect the spiritually dead. WOW! As the Lord spoke, He also showed me glimpses of my future. I became very afraid of the glimpses I had seen, because I knew I was not qualified to accomplish what He had shown me. God assured me not to worry. I fell to my knees and praised Him that night - in our yard, under the stars!

I ran back into the house, woke my husband up and told him about all the glorious things the Lord had revealed to me. My husband shared with me the Lord spoke with him in a similar manner when he was called to preach the Gospel. My husband surprised me when he stated he had known for a while I was also going to preach the Gospel. He said I had a strong anointing on my life, and it could not be hidden.

After our conversation, my husband set a date for me to preach my "Trial Sermon." In most black Baptist Churches, a Trial Sermon is when a person preaches his/her sermon in front of the Church, and then the Church agrees to license him/her as a Minster of the Gospel. That night, my husband and I shared a special moment that I will never forget. Although he was the cause of a lot of my tears, He was still willing to help me pursue my new calling. I was reminded of Romans 8:28 - "And we know that all things work together for good to them that love God, to them who are called according to his purpose."

I was exceptionally nervous the day of my Trial Sermon; but I knew the day was larger than me! I was on a mission to do God's will. God wanted to use me to fulfill His purpose and to aid others who may be going through "issues." He wanted to use me to help change lives. I could not have imagined in a million years that I would one day go from sitting on the last pew of the Church, to sitting in the pulpit about to deliver God's message. The feeling was surreal, to say the least! I was very afraid, but I was willing to be an empty vessel for the Lord. I wanted Him to use me in every way possible! That night God showed me the stars, He assured me I was able to take on the task ahead of me. I had no choice but to trust and believe Him! I was reminded of the times my husband and I used to sit in the car and gaze at the stars, before we were married. We did not know where those stars were going to lead us, but we trusted the God who made and placed them in the sky.

It was time for my Trial Sermon and I was elated my family had traveled from near and far to support me. The Church was packed to capacity. Everyone wanted to hear what I had to say. I fully intended to allow God to use me to deliver a message to His people - and that is exactly what I did! My sermon was entitled: "No Test, No Testimony." My scriptural reference was taken from the Book of Revelation – Revelation 12:9-11, to be exact.

"And they overcame him by the blood of the Lamb, and by the word of their testimony; and they loved not their lives unto the death." At that moment, I did not care what people had to say. I was not concerned about the latest rumor. I was not worried about what had happened, or what I had endured. That day, the Spirit of the Lord fell upon me and I was able to preach God's message with a boldness that I did not know was possible. I had a flashback of my first time being on stage, when I was in the Drama Club. That same Spirit came over me. As the people started to shout and applaud, I knew I had found my purpose. I realized God was preparing me, my entire life, for that moment! I had entered into my destiny! I was going to allow God to use my life by any means necessary.

Every tear I shed had a divine purpose. Every trial I endured had made me stronger. I was a living testimony of how God could transform a person's mess into a message and their troubles into triumphs. At that moment, I was no longer a victim of my circumstances - I was victorious over my circumstances. I was in control of my own life. Although, I could have let my troubles kill me, I chose to live through them and trust God's plan for my life. I chose life over death. What the devil meant for bad, God had worked out for my good.

As I reflect on my life, I have endured my fair share of pain and suffering, but I never endured it alone. God always sent someone my way; whether it was my daughter's angelic voice singing a simple song, a dear friend with a listening ear or three wise women who would not take "No" for an answer. God used people in my life to help me overcome adverse situations. Every time I felt I was at my lowest point, God sent someone to reveal His love through them. You can rest assured knowing God will never leave you, nor forsake you! You may not understand why you are going through what you are going through, but know that your tears are not in vain. In due season, God will use everything you have endured to help you discover your purpose and destiny!

We never know where life will take us. One minute, we can have our life planned out - living our dreams. The next minute, all hell can be breaking loose in our lives! Unfortunately, the devil will sometimes use people who are close to us to wreak havoc in our lives. The devil's main job is to steal, kill and destroy, and he will use anyone or anything to complete his mission. We are all human, which means we are not exempt from experiencing the pain or suffering that comes from unfortunate life circumstances. At a certain point, we must recognize the demons that dwell in others. The Bible tells us that we are not fighting against flesh and blood, but against spiritual wickedness in high places. Those evil spirits all have one common goal: They want to control our minds. If they can take control our minds, they will eventually take control of our bodies and cause us to do things we will later regret.

We all have choices in life. We must be mindful, the decisions we make can forever change the direction of our lives and the lives of those we love and cherish. We cannot control when a loved one's bad decisions bring negative circumstances in our lives. Although, we cannot control the occurrence of the negative circumstances, we can control the outcome of the negative circumstances! We can gain freedom by choosing to forgive. Forgiveness is not intended for the offending party - it is intended for you. Forgiveness does not mean you approve of what happened; it simply means you have given yourself permission to move forward with your life. On my journey, I have discovered adversity can either make you bitter or make you better. Through my sacred tears, I have chosen to become better! This is my testimony. By the grace of God...I AM VICTORIOUS!

Epilogue

Fanitra's spiritual maturation is commendable. Eight years ago, she singlehandedly held our family together after I foolishly and regrettably made a series of bad choices, which caused a chain of negative events to transpire in our lives. Fanitra stood by my side, when she had every reason and right to move forward without me. Her steadfast faith, in the midst of adversity, showed me the power of a praying wife. Fanitra's unwavering love was instrumental in leading me back to the road of redemption.

If you live long enough, you'll make mistakes. But if you learn from them, you'll be a better person. It's how you handle adversity, not how it affects you. The main thing is never quit, never quit, never quit. - President Bill Clinton

Sacred Tears is an incredibly transparent literary work, which documents how my wife used her pain to propel her into her purpose. The book addresses relatable issues such as joy & sorrow, marriage & infidelity, brokenness & wholeness, kinship & friendship and ultimately, the freedom of forgiveness. *Sacred Tears* is a must read; it is raw, real and relevant! –D.B.

About The Author

Lady Fanitra Brantley was born in 1980 in Atlanta, GA to the parentage of Leon and Myra (Hart) Roman. She accepted Jesus during her teen years and was formally licensed as a minister in 2010. She is currently in pursuit of becoming a licensed clinical psychologist.

In 1999, Lady Brantley was joined in Holy Matrimony to Rev. Darnell A. Brantley. Their union has produced four beautiful children - Zayla, Darnell Jr., Faith & Destiny.

Over the years, Lady Fanitra has faithfully served as the 1st Lady of three Missionary Baptist churches. While functioning in that capacity, she quickly realized God had anointed her to do mighty works for the Kingdom. Under Lady Fanitra's leadership, hundreds of people have dedicated their lives to the Lord, new churches have been constructed and numerous meaningful ministries have been established. Lady Fanitra is also the owner of *Birthday Bashes & Events* and a radio personality on WMQGRadio.com. Her clothing line, *Life & Style by Lady Fanitra*, will debut in 2016.

Lady Fanitra's love for Jesus and vibrant personality have made her a sought after Youth Director, preacher, teacher and motivational speaker. Her personality can only be mirrored by her passion. Lady Fanitra is passionate about "Changing Lives through Jesus Christ" by learning, loving and living God's Word!

Printed in the United States
By Bookmasters